The Shaphan Group

The Shaphan Group

The Fifteen Authors Who
Shaped the Hebrew Bible

PRESTON KAVANAGH

◈PICKWICK *Publications* · Eugene, Oregon

THE SHAPHAN GROUP
The Fifteen Authors Who Shaped the Hebrew Bible

Copyright © 2011 Preston Kavanagh. All rights reserved. Except for brief quotations in critical papers or reviews, no part of this book may be reproduced in any manner without prior written permission from the publisher. Write: Permissions, Wipf and Stock Publishers, 199 W. 8th Ave., Suite 3, Eugene, OR 97401.

Pickwick Publications
An Imprint of Wipf and Stock Publishers
199 8th Ave., Suite 3
Eugene, OR 97401

www.wipfandstock.com

Scripture quotations contained herein (unless otherwise noted) are from the New Revised Standard Version of the Bible, copyright © 1989 by the National Council of Churches of Christ in the USA. Used by permission. All rights reserved.

ISBN 13: 978-1-60608-611-7

Cataloguing-in-Publication data:

Kavanagh, Preston.

　The Shaphan group : the fifteen authors who shaped the Hebrew Bible / Preston Kavanagh.

　xii + 142 p.—Includes bibliographical references and index.

　ISBN 13: 978-1-60608-611-7

　1. Bible. O.T.—Criticism, interpretation, etc. 2. Ciphers in the Bible. 3. Bible. O.T.—Data processing. I. Title.

BS1197 K37 2011

Manufactured in the U.S.A.

This book is dedicated to the heroes and heroines who shaped the Hebrew Scriptures, including Shaphan (King Josiah's Secretary), Shaphan's three sons— Ahikam, Elasah, and Gemariah—and his father Azaliah; the scribes Baruch and Micaiah as well as Micaiah's son Achbor; the priestly brothers Ezra and Jozadak; the prophets Jacob and Jeremiah; the prophetess Huldah; Daniel; and also Asaiah, who held the title under Josiah of Servant to the King.

CONTENTS

Tables and Figures · viii
Preface · ix
Acknowledgments · x
Abbreviations · xi

1 The Basics of Coding · 1
2 Anagrams Uncover Priestly Source · 23
3 Ezra and Jozadak BAs Sketch Exile's History · 45
4 The Dtr Solution: Shaphan and His Group · 67
5 The Shaphan Group's Prodigious Output · 87

Appendix One—Shaphan Group's Coded Chapters in Scripture · 111
Appendix Two—Books of Scripture
    with Shaphan-Group Spellings =≤ .001 · 124
Bibliography · 127
Index of Subjects and Modern Authors · 131
Index of Hebrew Scripture · 139

TABLES AND FIGURES

Tables

1.1 Personal Names of High Value Concealed Within Priestly Benediction · 4
1.2 Ezra Athbash Variations · 13
1.3 Ezra-the-priest-the-scribe Athbash Spellings in Isaiah 3 · 14
2.1 Multiple BAs in Single Text Words · 30
4.1 Shaphan Anagrams in Genesis 1:1—2:4 · 72
4.2 Percent of DH Chapters Coded with Names of 15 Notables from Later Monarchy and Exile · 74
4.3 Examples of Huldah's Coding Expertise in Deuteronomy · 77
5.1 Coded Spellings: Shaphan Group's Impact on Deuteronomistic History · 88
5.2 Significant Signature Spellings by the Shaphan Group within Judges 12 · 90
5.3 Coded Spellings/Thousand Text Words: The Shaphan Group's Impact on Sections in the Book of Numbers · 92
5.4 Coded Spellings/Thousand Text Words: The Shaphan Group's Impact on Chapters in the Book of Numbers · 93
5.5 The Shaphan Group's Coded Chapters in Scripture (Excerpt from Appendix 1) · 99
5.6 Rank in Book of Isaiah Using Coded Groups among Fifteen Shaphan Members · 100
5.7 The Shaphan Group's Coded Chapters in Isaiah 40–55 (Excerpt from Appendix 1) · 102

Figure

The Shaphan Group in King Josiah's Time—620 BCE · 69

PREFACE

This writer has worked full-time on the authorship of the Hebrew Scriptures for twenty-four years—but not until after twenty-three and one-half years was the Shaphan-group discovery made. In retrospect, it seems likely that other things had to precede that finding. In rough chronological order these have been: Second Isaiah's identity, coded spelling, athbash multiplication, Ezra's proper era, Word Links, Babylon's use of substitute kings, the Suffering Servant's name, Jehoiachin's fate, anagrams, the Cyrus revolt, the P Source's name, and the Ezra-Jozadak rivalry. Other students of Scripture are, of course, unaware of this background. Understandably, they may be reluctant to accept the Shaphan-group breakthrough. In addition, such reluctance may be compounded by this author's frequent reliance upon tables and probabilities. Although these are not part of the traditional approach to biblical scholarship, *The Shaphan Group* also employs these techniques—we think to good advantage. Fellow students of the Bible can now discover the authors and dates of Isaiah, Psalms, Proverbs, Job, Songs, Daniel, and half of the Minor Prophets—as well as who edited the DH and part of the Pentateuch. As you pick up *The Shaphan Group*, we humbly urge your forbearance and ask for your attention.

ACKNOWLEDGMENTS

I thank K. C. Hanson, editor-in-chief at Wipf and Stock, for offering the opportunity to lay *Shaphan Group's* discoveries before biblical scholars, and Barbara Oldroyd for the editing skill and stylistic rigor that she applied to this text. Most especially, this writer is indebted to John Page, President of MultiMedia Communications, for his computer systems skills, and also to Bill Miller, Professor emeritus at Iowa State University. He developed and then cheerfully contributed the chi-square programs that John Page applies so successfully to Scripture. And, of course, I thank Lois, my wife, for her patience and understanding.

ABBREVIATIONS

ABD	*Anchor Bible Dictionary,* 6 vols., edited by David Noel Freedman. New York: Doubleday, 1992
Ant	Josephus *Antiquities*
AOAT	Alter Orient und Altes Testament
BA	biblical anagram
BASOR	*Bulletin of the American Schools of Oriental Research*
BCE	Before Common Era
BDB	*The New Brown-Driver-Briggs-Gesenius Hebrew and English Lexicon.* by Francis Brown et al. Peabody, MA: Hendrickson, 1979
Bib	*Biblica*
BR	*Bible Review*
CE	Common Era
DH	Deuteronomistic History
Dtr	Deuteronomistic Historian, seventh century
Dtr²	Deuteronomistic Historian, sixth century
EncJud	*Encyclopaedia Judaica,* corrected edition, 17 vols., edited by Cecil Roth and Geoffrey Wigoder. Jerusalem: Keter, 1972
HS	Hebrew Scripture
ID	Signature words used by Jacob the prophet
IDB	*Interpreter's Dictionary of the Bible,* 4 vols., edited by George A. Buttrick. Nashville, TN: Abingdon, 1962
J Source	Yahwist Source
JBL	*Journal of Biblical Literature*
JNES	*Journal of Near Eastern Studies*
JSB	Jewish Study Bible

Abbreviations

MT	Masoretic Text
NRSV	New Revised Standard Version
OT	Old Testament
P Source	Priestly Source
Parpola I	Simo Parpola, *Letters from Assyrian Scholars to the Kings Esarhaddon and Assurbanipal: Texts*, AOAT. Kevalaer: Butzon & Bercker, 1970
Parpola II	Simo Parpola, *Letters from Assyrian Scholars to the Kings Esarhaddon and Assurbanipal: Commentary and Appendices*, AOAT. Kevalaer: Butzon & Bercker, 1983
Sanh.	*Sanhedrin*
VTSup	Vetus Testamentum Supplements
ZAW	*Zeitschrift für die alttestamentliche Wissenschaft*
ZTK	*Zeitschrift für Theologie und Kirche*

1

The Basics of Coding

Coding and the Priestly Benediction

This could be an exciting time to study Scripture. For the first time, scholars have the means to wrest from ancient texts the deeper meanings that their authors intended. Armed with computers faster than lightning, those who work with the Bible can have a substantial advantage over such giants of interpretation as Jerome, Rashi, Luther, and Wellhausen. Learning, imagination, and diligence are never—will never be—out of date. But now biblical scholars can apply the freshly discovered approach of coding. A prior book illustrated that new technique.[1] This opening chapter will highlight the basics of coding and how it can be multiplied by athbash. The chapter also shall address a question many have raised: Is coding in Hebrew Scripture possible at all?

At the heart of biblical coding *is a simple technique. To encode a word*, the author used one letter from consecutive text words. To add flexibility, the extracted letters could run in any order. For example, the name "Patricia" can be found in the italicized words above: "*is a simple technique. To encode a word* . . ." The underlined sequence is i-a-p-i-t-c-a-r. The letters come from consecutive words. Because the letters in "Patricia" are common, it would take numerous coded spellings bunched within

---

1. Kavanagh, *Exilic Code*.

a shorter text to produce a statistically significant coding. This raises an important matter.

The aim of a coding search is to isolate and save important data while discarding the rest—wheat from chaff, if you will. The basis for doing this is probability. Search results from Scripture must be subject to probability tests. The probability cutoff this book employs excludes most coincidental findings. The exclusion line has been set at .001, or a probability of coincidence of one in one thousand. (It is odd that the lower the decimal, the greater the probability that the finding is *not* coincidental. In terms of *im*probability of coincidence, .001 is superior to .005.) The risk in using a conservative limit like .001 is that we shall pass over names in the text that biblical authors meant for their contemporaries to find. But all things considered, it is better to begin a new venture conservatively.

Among the best illustrations of coding in HS is the Priestly Benediction. The benediction will be familiar to every reader. In translation, it says, "The LORD bless you and keep you; the LORD make his face to shine upon you, and be gracious to you; the LORD lift up his countenance upon you, and give you peace."[2]

The Revised Standard Version concludes that these words were "undoubtedly" used in the Jerusalem temple (note to Num 6:22–27), which would date the benediction's composition no later than the seventh century BCE. However, the fifteen Hebrew words are stuffed with codings of the name "Jehoiachin." He was on Judah's throne when, in 587 BCE, Nebuchadnezzar took Jerusalem and transported the young Judahite king to Babylon. Scripture's last mention of Jehoiachin was when the Babylonians released him from prison, ostensibly to honor him but actually to slay him as a substitute king. Jehoiachin's martyrdom would have occurred on or before April 6 in 561.[3] Thus, the coded spellings allow us to date the Priestly Benediction as no earlier than 587, when Nebuchadnezzar forced Jehoiachin from the throne. More likely, an unknown author penned those words after the exiled king's death in 561. The passage is aptly named a benediction and probably commemorated the Judahite king's death.

---

2. Num 6:24–26. Unless otherwise noted, quotations in this book are from the New Revised Standard Version of the Bible.

3. Kavanagh, *Exilic Code*, 16–18.

The Basics of Coding

The benediction's first set of encodings consists of fourteen spellings of יויכן, "Jehoiachin." The first such spelling is shown below, and underlines show the letters employed. The pattern is one letter per text word, with letters taken from consecutive words. Sequence does not matter, and the letter order of this first spelling is כויייך.

²⁴ יְבָרֶכְךָ יְהוָה וְיִשְׁמְרֶךָ׃
²⁵ יָאֵר יְהוָה פָּנָיו אֵלֶיךָ וִיחֻנֶּךָּ׃
²⁶ יִשָּׂא יְהוָה פָּנָיו אֵלֶיךָ וְיָשֵׂם לְךָ שָׁלוֹם׃

In like manner, the expert who wrote Num 6:24–26 fit another thirteen Jehoiachin spellings into the confines of these spare Hebrew lines. The note gives the sequence, interval, and starting text word for the thirteen remaining codings.[4] The benediction's text, just fifteen words long, can accommodate fifteen coded spellings of six letters each (the two fifteens are coincidental). So יויכן scores fourteen spellings out of fifteen opportunities. The spellings/opportunities ratio for every Hebrew name has been calibrated beforehand, and such probability measures are in place before any search begins. In this case, the fourteen hits out of fifteen opportunities earn the Jehoiachin spelling an A—the top rating.

Hebrew personal names sometimes have spelling variations, and "Jehoiachin," with seven, has more than any. (One of these was inscribed upon a jar handle found in 1928 by W. F. Albright.[5] Although it does not appear in Scripture, that variation is encoded in the benediction.) The Jehoiachin versions, *along with all other Israelite and Judahite personal names in Scripture,* were also run against the words of the Priestly Benediction to see which might also have been encoded within that text. The results were highly unusual, as table 1.1 shows:

---

4. The letter sequence, (word interval), and starting text word for the other thirteen Jehoiachin spellings are: יויכן (2) 24-1, ויייני (1) 24-2, יינוך (2) 24-2, כויייי (1) 24-3, כויני (2) 24-3, יונכיי (1) 25-1, יניוך (2) 25-1, יכיניי (2) 25-2, נכוייי (1) 25-3, כנייי (1) 25-4, יינכו (1) 25-5, ייניוך (1) 26-1, and יניכו (1) 26-2.

5. Albright, "Seal of Eliakim," 81; Albright, "Joiachin in Exile," 50. The following challenge identifying יכן with Jehoiachin: Malamat, "Judah in the Maelstrom," 138 n 34; Ussishkin, "Private Seal Impressions," 11.

TABLE 1.1
Personal Names of High Value Concealed within Priestly Benediction

1	Cushi	כושי	A
2	Shecaniah	שכנייהו	A
3	Jehoiachin	יויכין	A
4	Jehoiachin	יכניה	A
5	Jehoiachin	יכוניה	A
6	Jehoiachin	כניהו	B
7	Jehoiachin	יהויכין	B
8	Jehoiachin	יוכן	B
9	Jecoliah	יכליהו	B

Of 1,302 Hebrew personal names found in Scripture, rabbinic writings, and archaeology, 65 percent could not have been coded in the benediction because they contained Hebrew letters that the benediction lacked. Searches with the 456 remaining names found but nine statistically significant Hebrew names, six of which were variations of Jehoiachin—three with A values and three with B values. The third name on the list is יויכין, which, as we saw earlier, formed fourteen spellings. The other five Jehoiachin versions had thirteen, fourteen, fifteen, ten, and twenty-one codings, respectively. In total, within the Priestly Benediction, "Jehoiachin" is encoded no fewer than eighty-seven times.[6] Among other biblical names, only Cushi, Shecaniah, and Jecoliah achieved ratios at the A or B level.

Could the six A and B "Jehoiachin" coding groups found within Num 6:24–26 have been coincidental? The answer is an emphatic no. Imagine a vat containing 456 balls, six of them red and the other 450 black. The odds are 1.7 million to one against pulling those six red balls (the Jehoiachin spellings) and just three black balls (the other three names) in nine draws from the vat.[7] And to make coincidence even less likely, Jehoiachin's name is closely linked with "Shecaniah," which is one

---

6. Details about all coded spellings are shown in Kavanagh, *Exilic Code*, 12, n 24 and n 25.

7. P = a combination of (9 choose 6) (447 choose 3) / 456 choose 9 = 5.72×10^{-10}. P is the probability of coincidence.

of the other three names. "Shecaniah" comes from a ration tablet found in Babylon that listed issues to the exiled Judahite king's household.[8] As to "Cushi" and "Jecoliah," Cushi might have been one of King Jehoiachin's exiled ministers, and Jecoliah, which is feminine, could have been the king's wife.

At this point, most would admit that the case for a biblical code is strong. Here is a restatement, with some additional facts thrown in. There are eighty-seven Jehoiachin spellings fashioned under the rules of only one letter per text word, from words at regular intervals, with spellings in any sequence. These spellings have all been verified by the experts who work at the Vatican journal *Biblica*. After such verification, that periodical published an article on Jehoiachin coding in the Priestly Benediction.[9] Then there is the matter of probabilities. The probability of coincidence that six of the nine significantly coded names would be variations of "Jehoiachin" is tiny—.000000000572. Interested readers can verify the underlying data without much difficulty.[10]

In the example of the Priestly Benediction, most of the eighty-seven coded spellings took letters from consecutive text words, while a few used every other word. For simplicity, in the rest of this book we shall use only spellings taken from consecutive text words, intentionally excluding those that employed letters from every second, third, fourth, or fifth text word. This consecutive-word approach is simpler and would have been easier for the ancients to decipher. Most biblical authors probably used this less cumbersome approach. Also, a tally of coding intervals puts one-interval spellings well ahead of those with multiple spaces.

Chi-Square Test

As other biblical scholars do, we deal with likelihood rather than certainty, which makes probability studies all the more necessary. The following explains how we apply probabilities for one-interval spellings. The ratio of

---

8. Weidner, "Jojachin," 923–35; cited by Albright, "King Jehoiachin," 51–52.

9. Kavanagh, "Jehoiachin Code," 234–44.

10. Tally Hebrew personal names in Scripture using a source like the *IDB*. Spelling variations count as separate names. Eliminate names containing any of the nine letters not present in Num 6:24–26. About 427 should remain, including six variations of "Jehoiachin." If you are in the neighborhood of 420-plus names, you have verified the test result. (The 456 figure in note 7 comes from adding twenty-nine rabbinic and archaeologically furnished names, a figure that it may not be possible to replicate.)

coded spellings to text words within a chapter will be compared with that same ratio throughout the rest of Scripture. To these two independent sets of figures, using the computer, we apply a chi-square test. The test asks the question: What is the probability that chance alone produces x coded spellings in a chapter the size of y, given that $x1$ coded spellings occur in the remainder of Scripture's words ($y1$)? The smaller the probability, the less chance there is that the chapter's spellings are due to coincidence. For example, assume that 9,180 spellings occur in the Bible's 305,496 text words and that our chapter contains 24 spellings in 300 words. The ratios to compare are 24 spellings/300 text words and 9,156 spellings/305,196 text words. Applying the chi-square test, we find the probability that the chapter's 24 spellings could have been due to chance alone is .000002, or about one chance in a half-million. Remembering that low is good, the spellings in this hypothetical chapter would be well below our .001 probability standard. We would judge that the author intentionally inserted those spellings in the text. The technique is simple, effective, and—with a computer—quickly and easily applied.

Coding offers experts an entirely different way to get at questions of editing and textual breaks. In the Priestly Benediction, for example, coding within the benediction tends to confirm that this fifteen-word masterpiece is an original unedited piece, and that it is about the exiled King Jehoiachin. The three short verses of the benediction are set within three other verses—two at the start and one at the conclusion. Though stilted and amateurish when compared to the benediction, these other verses convey important clues about Jehoiachin's fate.

The Assyrians regularly used the word *sarpuhi* to designate a substitute king, and the benediction's framing verses use coding to document that Jehoiachin died as a substitute in Babylon.[11] These added verses expand the coded spellings of "Jehoiachin-sarpuhi" from twenty-three within the benediction to thirty-five when all six verses that end Num 6 are used.[12] Also, the new verses increase the values of the coding sets from A-A-A-B-D-E, using only the benediction's fifteen words, to A-A-

---

11. The Assyrians and the Neo-Babylonians used substitute kingship extensively. It is likely that Jehoiakim, Jehoiachin, Zedekiah, and Ezekiel—who was the Suffering Servant—died as substitute kings of Babylon. See Kavanagh, *Exilic Code*, 49–51, 107, and 110.

12. See table 1.3 in Kavanagh, *Exilic Code*, 16. In every encoded spelling in Num 6:22–27, the word שׁפרוּהי is preceded by one of the six versions of "Jehoiachin."

A-A-A-A when also employing the framing verses. Clearly, these biblical editors possessed a working knowledge of coding and well understood how to enhance original coded spellings.

In addition to coding enhancements, the benediction's framing verses offer clues as to authorship and dating. (Anagrams are involved and, for now, readers should think of them as coding within a single text word.) Those verses read, "The LORD spoke to Moses, saying: Speak to Aaron [Ezra anagram] and his sons, saying, Thus you shall bless [Baruch anagram] the Israelites: You shall say to them . . ." The benediction follows. The closing verse is, "So they shall put my name on the Israelites, and I will bless them" (Num 6:22–23, 27). As we shall explain in chapter 2, "Aaron" is an anagram for "Ezra," and "bless" is an anagram for "Baruch." Also, "Israelites," which occurs twice, could identify Second Isaiah, whose name was "Jacob."[13] (In Scripture, the prophet used "Jacob" and "Israel" interchangeably.) One could speculate that Jacob wrote the benediction soon after Jehoiachin's death, and that Baruch and Ezra later added the three framing verses, scattering clues as they did so.

The benediction itself conceals at least two anagrams. Its eighth word is ויחנך, which has the letters יוכן, a Jehoiachin version. The Jehoiachin anagram is in addition to the eighty-seven coded spellings of Jehoiachin that we have already noted, so the anagram itself tells us nothing different about the subject of this short passage. There is, however, a second anagram within the benediction that could shed light on Jehoiachin's death. At the end of Num 6:24 is the word וישמרך, "and keep you," which contains an anagram for כורש, "Cyrus." This offers the possibility that Jehoiachin was killed because of his relationship with the Persian. Triangulations like these can help to date passages, establish authorship, and reconstruct historical events. Based only upon coding and anagrams, the benediction seems to have been written during the decade following Jehoiachin's death in April of 561 BCE. If Baruch and Ezra did indeed add the enclosing verses, they might have composed them when the original author—possibly Jacob—was no longer able to write. Far from prohibiting coding interpretation, the fact that we are not working with an "original" text can be an advantage. Coding changes within an edited text can tell us much about the ancient times we seek to understand.

---

13. See Kavanagh, *Exilic Code*, 62–84.

The connection between coding and establishing dates bears emphasis. A coded word carries no date stamp—it is neutral as to time. However, the word can set an upper limit for a passage's composition. For example, because Josiah preceded the Babylonian king, a verse encoded with "Nebuchadnezzar" should not be assigned to Josiah's time. On the other hand, since the author might be retelling an older story, we cannot offhandedly conclude that the verse was composed during Nebuchadnezzar's reign.

To encode a name, one can take letters from the next text word, or from every second, or third, or fourth, or fifth word. But a longer compound (like "Ezra-the-priest-the-scribe" with a five-word interval) can require over seventy text words to deliver a single coded spelling. That probably would have asked too much of ancient scribes—or of modern credulity. One can achieve virtually the same end by counting only spellings derived from consecutive text words. Though probabilities work equally well with either system, this book will use the shorter approach.

Nevertheless, even probabilities have vagaries. For example, different letters of the Hebrew alphabet have widely different rates of occurrence. The name Micaiah, מיכיה, contains common Hebrew letters. Probably as a result, Gen 1 encodes Micaiah twenty-five times, and Scripture as a whole contains more than twenty thousand such spellings. At the other extreme is כחטנג, which is an athbash variant of Micaiah (more on athbash later). In all of HS there are but two coded spellings of this unusual combination. The scarcity of כחטנג makes each of those occurrences statistically significant, while מיכיה coding is so commonplace that we should ignore the twenty-five spellings in Gen 1. (Genesis 1 would need double that number of spellings to achieve significance.) With this start, we are ready to consider the problems that coding presents.

Coding in an Imperfect Bible

After hearing of biblical codes, some skeptical scholars argue that it is next to impossible to recover Scripture's original words. One told me that we are dealing with a "medieval text," by which he presumably referred to the Leningrad Codex (1008 CE) and the Aleppo Codex (925 CE). Another scholar wrote that "in order for such decoding to be accurate, one must assume that that we can identify the exact wording of the original text, something no biblical scholar who knew anything about text criticism can accept." This line of reasoning skips probabilities (like the .000000000572) and challenges presuppositions. There cannot be coding beneath the Hebrew text, they hold, because we can never be sure that we are working with the original text.

They make a point. There are gaps of hundreds of years when scribes and clerks would have recopied the great-great-great (add as many as you like) grandchildren of the original writing, and therefore had countless opportunities to err or alter. I have used the MT's Leningrad Codex, the source that many scholars and at least one commercial search program also employ. Probably most of that version is "original"; some part of it undoubtedly is not. As my email critic properly points out, we can never be absolutely certain that the text being examined is original and unedited.

However, the answer to that is twofold. First, the Qumran discoveries—particularly of the complete Isaiah scroll—have reduced by a thousand years the gap between the time when Scripture was composed and the time when the medieval manuscripts were written. Painstaking examination of these texts and Qumran's Isaiah scroll has "revealed the remarkable accuracy with which scribes copied the sacred texts . . . When scholars compared the MT of Isaiah to the Isaiah scroll of Qumran, the correspondence was astounding."[14] For an example, focusing on whatever might affect coded spellings in Isa 53, only seventeen of the chapter's 667 letters showed any differences—a disparity of less than 3 percent. Another scholar found that the Isaiah scrolls "proved to be word for word identical with our standard Hebrew Bible in more than 95 percent of the text."[15] Millar Burrows wrote, "It is a matter of wonder that . . . the text underwent so little alteration."[16]

The second thing that should allay doubts about coding is simple, and we think compelling. The text we have is the text we have, and there is overwhelming statistical proof that what we have contains coding. It does not always have to be coding inserted by an original author. A biblical editor or an editor's editor might have put it there.[17] It might even have been implanted by medieval hands—though this is almost beyond imagining.

14. Brantley, "Biblical Integrity," 25–30.
15. Archer, *Survey*, 25. Quoted by Zukeran, "Scrolls."
16. Burrows, *Dead Sea Scrolls*, 304. Quoted by Zukeran, "Scrolls."
17. Coding by editors can also yield helpful information (see the earlier Priestly Benediction discussion).

The Shaphan Group

What will letter changes, word deletions, and word insertions do to coding already present in a text? Pretend that the "Micaiah" coding in Gen 1 was intentional. The chapter had thirteen single spellings employing five text words each, two double spellings using six consecutive words apiece, and a pair of four-in-a-row spellings that both required eight of the chapter's text words to complete. In all, ninety-three of the chapter's 434 text words supplied a letter to coded letter chains. Thus, changes in a text's words or letters have only about one chance in five of affecting any of the Micaiah spellings (93/434). Moreover, given that Hebrew words average about four letters, a clerical error that changed just one character would have only a one-in-four chance of altering the single letter used to build the spelling. And while a deletion or an insertion in the middle of any spelling string would shorten (or even end) it, the chances of destroying more than a single Micaiah coding are about two-to-one against. Assuming that the distribution of Micaiah coding in Gen 1 is reasonably typical, the damage over time to most of an originator's coding should not be heavy. And in many instances there will be no damage at all. Besides, textual changes would nearly always destroy coding rather than add new spellings. We simply would not find whatever used to be there.

My experience has been that most chapters in Scripture contain at least modest coding and that some chapters teem with it.[18] This means that virtually every textual change will disturb some coding. Still, the system's design is sturdy. The spellings are generally short, do not depend upon long runs of text, and are usually capable of surviving scribal error. And since we cannot take the measure of what once was there, we must be satisfied with applying probabilities to what survives.

Would minor changes have introduced added coded spellings? Not often, though a clever editor might achieve something by switching one or more letters between adjacent words. How about scribal errors? Could they have introduced different coding? Although almost anything is possible, the conclusion should be no. Because coded words usually depend upon repetition, there is almost no chance that scribal error could have originated new or continued previous spellings.

Did editors add their own coded spellings by inserting text? Indeed they did, though only if their insertions had sufficient text words to ac-

---

18. See the chapter "Coding Revelations of Psalm Fifty-One" in Kavanagh, *Exilic Code*, 85–106. Appendix 3 of that book details over 800 specific coded spellings within this short psalm.

commodate spellings. However, where they either initiated codes or supplemented those already in place, decoding searches can find them. The Priestly Benediction offers a perfect example of how sympathetic editors strengthened an originator's coding. The editors' three framing verses around Num 6:23–25 lifted the values of the "Jehoiachin" coding sets from A-A-A-B-D-E, using only the benediction's words, to A-A-A-A-A-A. Clearly those editors knew what they were doing.

Do letter substitutions and word changes prohibit codes within Scripture? No, they do not. The simplicity of the code makes it capable of surviving most textual alterations. But that is beside the point. Although the text we have undoubtedly contains numerous alterations, it still produces an avalanche of previously hidden names. In *this* book, coding governed by probabilities empowers us to identify a Dtr writer (for the first time ever), name Priestly Source authors, and detect the names of those who wrote hundreds of Scripture's chapters. That Scripture includes one of the Major Prophets and half of the Minor Prophets, as well as Job, Psalms, Proverbs, and Songs among the Writings. Does any current text do more?

Although the rewards are great, coding is not without problems, both ancient and modern.

Coding depended upon knowledge of secrets like athbash and anagrams. Catastrophes such as fire, plague, earthquake, persecution, and enemy conquest could extinguish any single group of experts, and snap chains of teaching. Eventually, this seems to have happened.

Coding was best done among contemporaries who knew the crises of the day and the identities of encoders. For example, who besides contemporaries would know that within Pss 104–7 are ciphers for Asaiah-servant-of-the-king, Daniel-the-eunuch, Ezra-the-priest-the-scribe, Jacob-son-of-Shelomoth, and Jozadak-son-of-Seraiah? Such mouth-to-ear knowledge probably disappeared quickly, and we are left to find—by trial and retrial—what once was secretly understood.

Coded words have no date, although sometimes they can establish a range of years from encoded associations. For example, finding Shecaniah and Jehoiachin together in the Priestly Benediction, we could guess an exilic text with a locus of Babylon. But often, coded names can surface that bear no relation to the text or to other names. Hezekiah mingles with Shaphan and Moses with Baruch. For these it is best to suspend judgment. Occasionally this turns out well, as when Ezra proves to be a contemporary of Second Isaiah rather than of Nehemiah. But for many such curiosities, there often is no present answer. As to specific dates for texts, I think it highly likely that biblical authors had an agreed-upon dating system. Perhaps by applying coding and athbash techniques someone else can find it.

Coding makes no distinction between author and subject. Sometimes the text's tone (like coding beneath a verbal attack) will make one or the other obvious, but usually not. Other coded passages within the chapter or in adjacent chapters may clarify, but this author-subject confusion will be a continuing problem.

Coding can produce too much data. True. For example, Daniel has stronger coding across more Proverbs chapters than others. Because of this, he is the leading prospect to be the book's author. But why does a single chapter, Prov 14, contain eight other significantly coded names after testing just forty alternatives? What will the Proverbs list look like after trying twelve hundred more personal names? Daniel's coding will not disappear, but others are certain to join him.

Coding exactingly answers only what is asked. Being one letter off can yield a B value instead of an AAA, or perhaps no value at all. Exilic encoders loved to use father-son combinations, but what does one do with "Jeiel," a common name shared by nine people with nine fathers?

We apply modern probability theories to ancient writings. Chi-square testing discards about 96 percent of Scripture's coding, which allows one to focus on unusual concentrations in the remaining 4 percent. However, using probability to draw the line between intention and coincidence can induce tunnel vision. We urge future analysts to add other approaches that delve in other directions. Those who wrote Scripture certainly lacked modern theories of probability, but they had lifetimes of experience in both coding and *de*coding. Also, they could identify rarer letter combinations and were skilled in marrying underlying coding with Scripture's surface words. Coding forms one part of Hebrew Scripture's cryptography. Another, which scholars have termed "athbash," follows.

The Athbash Expansion

In Jer 51:41, the writer uses the words ששך, "Sheshach," and בבל, "Babylon," interchangeably. The author derived the one from the other by first exchanging ב for ל and then ש for ב.

Athbash Letter Array of ששך = בבל

אבגדהוזחטיב
↑   ↓
תשרקפעסנמל

In the top line of the athbash array, Hebrew characters run from right to left, and in the bottom line they go from left to right. This scripturally based code is called "athbash" because *aleph* becomes *taw* and *beth* becomes *sin*. The key to multiplying athbash results is to rotate the two lines of letters, something that no other modern interpreter has discovered. The first rotation moves ת, the final letter of the alphabet, so that it stands next to א, which is the opening letter. The new array puts different characters opposite each other, and now spells בבל as קקט. Further rotations (with the eventual substitution of קקט as the base word) produce twenty more variations, for a total of twenty-one alternate spellings of the original בבל.

Table 1.2 gives readers a graphic view of the power that athbash expansion lent to Scripture's expert encoders. Using athbash, they would have had more than twenty times as many options in choosing words to tell two stories—the surface one and the one below the text. The table shows variations of the name עזרא, "Ezra," who was one of the Bible's most important writers.

TABLE 1.2
Ezra Athbash Variations

איקע	טצחב	פדמי
בסוט	יאנף	צמטנג
גלשץ	כרזד	קוסל
דפחך	לנעק	רכבה
הנאר	מתטו	שחפן
וקים	נהצץ	תמדז
זעגת	סבכח	
חשלם	עזרא	

The Shaphan Group

Athbash is mindless. The athbash process produces sets of commonly used letters like וקים and infrequently found ones like זעגת. The name "Ezra" has but four Hebrew letters, quite short by biblical encoding standards. Scripture's authors generally preferred to encode longer spellings—conglomerations of words that usually had been hinted at in Scripture itself. "Ezra-the-priest-the-scribe," spoken of above, is one such example. Those words occur together in Neh 8:9 and 12:26. The compound word that served as the basis of the athbash counterparts is עזראהכהנהספר. Isaiah 3, one of the most heavily coded chapters in the Bible, contains numerous Ezra-the-priest-the-scribe spellings. So that readers might more easily understand about separating coded wheat from chaff, table 1.3 lists the eight athbash variations represented within Isa 3.

TABLE 1.3
Ezra-the-priest-the-scribe Athbash Spellings in Isaiah 3

	Athbash Word	Spellings	Value
1	בסוטמקממתמאגו	1	
2	הנארעיעזעודא	7	
3	וקימפאפדפהזי	4	AAA
4	טצהברנרכרריחה	1	AAA
5	יאנפשהשחשטכן	2	
6	כרזדתעתמתלי ז	2	AAA
7	פדמיותוקוצעם	19	
8	שחפנידיאיתרף	18	A

The Isaiah chapter contains eight coded versions of Ezra-the-priest-the-scribe. Before these variations were run, they were tested against a large random sample of HS. In simple terms, the best passage in the large sample established the A value, and AA and AAA ratings were derived from that. All subsequent searches then tested for these pre-set values.[19]

Table 1.3 contains three AAA groups, one A value, and four groups that had no value at all. The formations in items 3 and 4 (the ו and ט athbash versions) are the most unusual. The large sample that set their

---

19. In later chapters of this book, a somewhat revised method will be applied.

pre-established AAA values found not a single spelling of them. Item 7 is the ס athbash. Its letters are common and its nineteen spellings are widely spread across the chapter. Statistically, we are free to ignore all those spellings. To push the word in item 8 (the ש athbash) to the A level, the authors of Isa 3 strung together six consecutive one-interval spellings. Although item 8 had eighteen spellings within the chapter, only the solid group of six has statistical significance.

Generalizing, every word to be searched has pre-established, statistically based, Bible-wide values based on rarity and concentration. The search itself considers all the spellings in a text, and then selects or rejects them based on those pre-established values. The same process was used for other Ezra-related word sets. These included Ezra, Ezra-son-of-Seraiah (with and without a final ו), Ezra-the-priest, Ezra-the-scribe, and Ezra-the-priest-the-scribe. After athbash expansion, these six Ezra-related search words with all their variations totaled 132 (22 athbash versions × 6).

The Ezra words still had another hurdle to jump. The computer searched every chapter in Scripture for Ezra words and assigned points to the values it found. (Scripture contained 10,680 points for those encodings.) Once in this form and matched with chapter lengths, the data became amenable to probability analysis. The probability that this Ezra-group concentration in Isa 3 was due solely to coincidence is essentially zero (62 points in 249 text words).[20]

Readers might conclude that such heavy coding identifies Ezra as the author of Isa 3. Based on the chapter's encodings, he might be. But mention, even statistically significant mention, does not an author make. All we know at this point is that the author of Isa 3 intentionally gave Ezra coded prominence. He certainly is a subject of Isa 3, but without concurring evidence we should not decide that Ezra wrote the chapter. The subject-author problem will continue to trouble practitioners of this art. However, those who decoded Scripture in biblical times most certainly confronted the same question. Perhaps authors encoded "written by x" or something similar into their texts. The matter awaits skilled modern attention.

---

20. The chi-square proportions are 62 / 10,618 and 249 / 304,652. P = 1.13 × 10^{-58}. The first proportion consists of coding points in Isa 3 and in the rest of Scripture, while the second has the text words in the same categories.

The Shaphan Group

The prophet Jacob (Second Isaiah's name) offers another example of how useful multiple coded words can be in tracking an individual. Jacob, sons-of-Jacob, house-of-Jacob, Jacob-the-prophet, and Jacob-son-of-Shelomoth have all served well.[21] Since Scripture's Jacob also called himself Israel, that name has been paired with those above. Israel-son-of-Shelomoth seems to work especially well. Neither Jacob-son-of-Isaac nor Israel-son-of-Isaac has been productive.

I have had relatively little experience in searching for longer phrases or shorter sentences. For one thing, until very recently, the search program had a fifteen-word limit. However, the modernized Code Finder program that may soon be generally available probably will have no such limitation. Those wishing to use the program to explore lengthier messages should by all means do so. There is a problem, however. At least so far, the coding software answers only what is asked of it. One must be specific as to the letters to be searched. It is with good reason that when searching for Ezra-son-of-Seraiah I spelled "Seraiah" both with and without a final ו. When searching other pairs with יה and יהו endings, I have often gotten an A value for one and AAA for the other, which indicates that the originator intended to encode the letters producing the higher value. Decoders must be exacting, and it is harder to be so with a fifteen-letter search term than with one containing ten or fewer characters.

The best result obtained with a longer phrase is with Jeremiah's-book-of-the-law, ספרהתורהלירמיהו. The word is encoded ninety-nine times in 2 Chr 34. The Chronicles chapter relates the discovery of the book of the law that prompted King Josiah's reforms. Identical though less numerous coding underlies the text of 2 Kgs 22. It tells the same story as 2 Chr 34, but with different (and earlier) words.[22] The Jeremiah coding points to a solution of this important book's source, and it could also offer clues about the identity of the Deuteronomistic Historian.

Several scholars have suggested to me that decoding Scripture without computers was too arduous for the ancients to perform. It does seem difficult. However, what else can account for the identical coding of

---

21. In seeking the name of Jacob's father, I used an eighty-chapter sample to explore possibilities. Ezekiel 22 contained AAA values for two athbash versions of יעקבבנשלמות. These could not have been coincidental. Moreover, Jacob-son-of-Shelomoth has consistently furnished better coding results than any other Jacob-related search term.

22. See Kavanagh, *Exilic Code*, 152–54.

Jeremiah's-book-of-the-law in both Second Kings and Second Chronicles? This coding lies beneath the parallel accounts of Josiah's reforms, and is even stronger in Chronicles than in Kings. At least one century separates composition of the two books.[23] Coding makes it certain that those who wrote Chronicles knew of Jeremiah's role in the reforms. Oral tradition probably played its part, but the evidence is that the Chronicler had a good grasp of *de*coding.

Made-up words help to illustrate coding. One is Jehoiachin-Sarpuhi, ייכינשרפוהי. The word *sarpuhi,* found in the Assyrian archives, comes from the cuneiform term for substitute king.[24] After learning by means other than coding that Jehoiachin had died as a substitute king, I thought it possible that *sarpuhi* was coded in the Priestly Benediction. I ran several Hebrew spellings of *sarpuhi* against a randomly drawn sample and then investigated the passages with good coding concentrations. Eventually, a promising Hebrew spelling surfaced, one that performed especially well in the Priestly Benediction ("Jehoiachin-sarpuhi" has thirty-five coded spellings in the benediction and its framing verses).

With "Jeremiah's-book-of-the-law," ספרהתורהלירמיהו, the approach skipped the random sample and concentrated on 2 Chr 34 and 2 Kgs 22. Although other tries yielded nothing, these attempts succeeded. Experimentation sometimes leads to discovery.

Why Hebrew Authors Used Coding

Scholars often ask why Hebrew authors used coding. The foremost answer is because the peoples around them did. Concealing secrets within writings was commonly practiced in the ancient world. Historian David Kahn says that cryptography in writing appears spontaneously when civilization reaches a certain level.[25] He attributes this to a general need for privacy. Egyptians, Arameans, Neo-Babylonians, Indians, Greeks, and Romans were among those who practiced the arts of cryptography. A previous writing documents this extensive use.[26]

---

23. Klein, "Chronicles," 995; Holloway, "Kings," 72.
24. Parpola I and Parpola II. The excursus in Part II discusses *sarpuhi.*
25. Kahn, *Codebreakers,* 84.
26. Kavanagh, *Exilic Code,* 1–2.

A Mesopotamian tablet dating from 1500 BCE employed special writing symbols to guard pottery-glazing secrets.[27] Neo-Babylonian scribes often used a cryptogram substituting numbers for characters when affixing their names to documents.[28] The *Kama Sutra*, an early Hindu work, listed coding and deciphering as arts women should practice.[29] An Indian text from the fourth century BCE advised ambassadors to employ cryptanalysis to obtain intelligence.[30] Both Augustus and Julius Caesar used ciphers.[31] A system in which letters are replaced by others further down the alphabet is still known as a Caesar code.[32] A lengthy fourth-century BCE Egyptian papyrus written in demotic script proved to have been an Aramaic cryptogram pertaining to a Syrian mystery cult.[33] In the fifth century BCE the Spartans used batons called skytales of varied thicknesses.[34] The sender wrote his message on a strip of parchment or leather wrapped around the baton, and the recipient decoded it by winding the strip around a skytale of the same thickness.

In using coding and anagrams, the OT authors were in good company. This book will trace coding use to the late monarchy, when a group associated with King Josiah wrote most of the psalms and much else. Since secret writing was well developed by the late seventh century, it is quite possible that earlier writers like Isaiah and perhaps even the J Source were also masters of that art. From the beginning, those who wrote Scripture worked under despots, which was reason enough to secrete information. The Talmud says that Isaiah was sawn to death by King Manasseh (*Sanh.* 10:2, 28c); Jeremiah fled for his life from King Jehoiakim (Jer 36:26); and Ezekiel as a substitute king was beheaded in Babylon.[35] During the opening decades of the sixth century, the Jews went from being a settled people with a central priesthood and sanctuary to groups scattered around the Ancient Near East. Coding within Scripture was a useful way to inform

---

27. Gadd and Thompson, "Middle-Babylonian Text," 87–96.
28. Leichty, "Colophon," 152.
29. *Kama Sutra*, under Study of Arts and Sciences: Intellectual Pastimes.
30. Shamasastry, *Kautilya's Arthasastra*, I, 12:21, 16:31.
31. Suetonius "Julius" 56; "Augustus" 88.
32. Kahn, *Codebreakers*, 84.
33. Bowman, "Text in Cryptogram," 219–27.
34. Plutarch, *Lives*, "Lysander," 19.
35. Kavanagh, *Exilic Code*, 107–21.

the Diaspora without disturbing authorities. Because so much of the OT was written during and after Josiah's reign, coding has an immense amount to reveal about the times that gave birth to Scripture.

During the Exile, for instance, coding and anagrams were employed to convey confidential news of a revolt in Palestine and then to lay blame for the disaster that followed. Ezekiel crammed eight Cyrus biblical anagrams into two short verses about a predator fouling pasture reserved for the owner's flock (Ezek 34:18–19). The Cyrus debacle, which probably occurred in the later 570s, is at present completely unrecognized by scholars.[36]

This next instance of confidential disclosure via a surface text may be the best of its kind in Scripture. The closing verses of Second Kings relate how—on a specific date—the Babylonian monarch released King Jehoiachin from prison, gave him new clothes, set him on a high throne, had him dine regularly at the king's table, and provided him a regular allowance "as long as he lived" (2 Kgs 25:27–30). At face value, the text was hopeful. Jehoiachin's release suggested the possible restoration of David's line in Judah. But face value revealed less than the truth. Instead, the real story the passage told was that, less than a week after Jehoiachin left prison, authorities beheaded him—the barbarous act that climaxed Babylon's substitute king ritual. The biblical author used some 470 word associations with other passages (Word Links) to describe this shocking outcome.[37] Word of mouth surely preceded the written account of Jehoiachin's death, and the news would quickly have traveled the length and breadth of the Diaspora. This means that literate Jews receiving the text would have known immediately that it mocked Babylon. They would have tested the verses for coding, anagrams, and Word Links to verify the real circumstances of their king's death.

Although these secret techniques were lost long ago, it is time that we set about recovering them. Unless we do, we shall continue to overlook the inner meaning of much of Scripture. We children of the twenty-first century should not underrate the achievements of those in the classical world. The recovery of the Antikythera Mechanism is a case in point.

---

36. Kavanagh, *Exilic Code*, 33–37.

37. A Word Link connects two passages that contain the same unique batch of words. Kavanagh, *Exilic Code*, devotes a full chapter and an appendix to Jehoiachin's martyrdom (see 42–61 and 174–76).

The Shaphan Group

The Antikythera Mechanism

In 1901, Greek sponge divers working off the small Aegean island of Antikythera recovered a shoebox-sized lump of bronze from the debris of a wreck twenty fathoms below the surface. Evidence from coins, amphorae, and other salvage showed that the sinking had occurred around the first half of the first century BCE. The ship and its lump of bronze had lain beneath the sea for two thousand years. Exposure to the air caused the bronze to split into pieces, revealing inscriptions in ancient Greek along with precisely cut sets of gear teeth. This seemed impossible, because such precise gearing had not been known until it appeared in medieval clocks some fourteen hundred years later.[38] Researcher John Seabrook writes that "Looking back over the first fifty years of research on the Mechanism, one is struck by the reluctance of modern investigators to credit the ancients with technological skill."[39]

Until the mid-1950s, the theory was that the box was an astrolabe—a navigating instrument used both in Hellenistic and Islamic times to determine latitude. Others, however, thought that the Antikythera Mechanism was far too advanced to be an astrolabe. Eventually, scholar Derek Price used X-rays to determine that the device was more sophisticated than anything previously known. He called it an ancient "computer." In 1974 he published "Gears from the Greeks." He concluded that nothing of this sophistication could have appeared full-blown without a preceding history of development, and he expected that attitudes would change toward ancient Greek technology.

But the academic world took little notice. Otto Neugebauer's huge *History of Ancient Mathematical Astronomy* came out the following year and allotted a single footnote to the Mechanism. As one expert told *New Yorker* author John Seabrook, "Classical scholarship is very literary, and focuses on texts—such as the writing of Homer, Sophocles, Virgil, or Horace . . . So when an archeological discovery about ancient technology arrives, it does not fit, because it's new, it's scientific, and it's not a text."

---

38. Perhaps the gear technology of the Greeks was kept alive by the Arabs and transmitted to Europe via Spain in the late Middle Ages. Seabrook, "Fragmentary Knowledge," 9.

39. Seabrook, "Fragmentary Knowledge," 4.

Another scholar concluded, "The Antikythera mechanism dropped and sank—twice—once in the sea and once in scholarship."

Academic jealousies hobbled further research on the Mechanism into the late nineteen-nineties, but finally, in 2005, X-rays taken with enhanced technology were able to see into the encrusted fragments. The results were stunning. "They took your breath away," said Tony Freeth, a leader of the project.[40] As the work now stands, there are several thousand characters and inscriptions, a nineteen-year calendar, and an eclipse-prediction cycle produced by a four-turn spiral of 223 lunar months.[41] A subsidiary dial even linked complex calendars used by astronomers to the civil calendars that regulated the four-year cycles of the Olympiad and the Pan-Hellenic games.[42]

For the Antikythera Mechanism, erroneous scholarly preconceptions cost dearly. Is the situation comparable in biblical studies? It is if my own twenty-three-year experience is the measure. Perhaps the best-known American biblical scholar told me as I attempted to explain coding that I was "chasing a chimera." We never even got to discuss probabilities. Another whose name and institution would be familiar said, after I told him that I had identified Second Isaiah, "It can't be in there. I would have found it if it were." I was then ushered out of his office. More recently, I have run into arguments stating that we cannot rely upon either probabilities or Scripture itself and that the ancients would have been unable to decode coding. On the plus side, a few scholars have been most supportive.[43]

The Word Link, coding, athbash, and biblical anagram discoveries—all supported by probabilities—will, in good time, transform biblical research. But let us hope that this will not require an additional hundred years. Upon reflection, however, I must add that so far biblical scholarship has lost virtually no time in capitalizing on these coding discoveries. This is because I have needed over twenty years to make and correct mistakes, organize the search and probability systems, write three books, and ready computer programs for the use of others. The technology is

40. Seabrook, "Fragmentary Knowledge," 10.
41. Freeth et al, "Calendars on the Antikythera Mechanism," 614.
42. Ball, "Complex Clock," 561.
43. Supportive scholars include Simo Parpola of the University of Helsinki and Horacio Simian-Yofre of Pontifical Biblical Institute.

transferable and may soon be widely available. One hopes that scholarly attention will follow.

The next chapter will use biblical anagrams to solve one of Scripture's enduring mysteries—the date and identity of the Priestly Source.

2

Anagrams Uncover Priestly Source

Biblical Anagrams

So far we have outlined coding and its expansion by athbash. These two techniques are fundamental to the new research approach. There is a third discovery that has equal standing—the anagram. Webster's says that an anagram is a word or sentence formed by transposing the letters of another word or sentence. As commonly understood, an anagram uses all the letters of the original in forming the anagram. For example, "orchestra" is an anagram of "carthorse."

Biblical writers, however, took a slightly different tack. The anagrams they fashioned might or might not use every letter of a text word. Thus, the name "Ezra," עזרא, could be an anagram taken from "Eleazer," אלעזר, even though "Ezra" uses only four of Eleazer's five letters. For illustration, anagrams formed from the English word "scripture" include put, rip, cure, pure, ripe, rite, sure, trip, true, erupt, script, and picture, among others. One can call this type of anagram a biblical anagram, or BA for short. *The biblical anagram is a Hebrew word or phrase formed by transposing some or all of the letters of another Hebrew word, using either athbash or true spellings.*

Biblical anagrams should substantially alter the way we conduct research in Hebrew Scripture, and may prove to be even more important than coding. Among other things, anagrams are less subject to textual changes than coded spellings. Anagrams are formed from a single text word rather than strings of words. As such, scribal errors and editorial deletions have far fewer chances of spoiling specific anagrams. A biblical composer had only to pick vocabulary that accommodated his BAs, and his or her readers needed only to be on the lookout for pre-understood text words.

English, Greek, Aramaic, and most other languages are better suited for anagrams than was biblical Hebrew, which averaged only 3.8 letters per word. This effectively limited Scripture's writers to encoding three- and four-letter names within single text words. A good example is that even after including athbash variations, all of Scripture yielded only five BAs of "Ezekiel," which has six Hebrew letters. "Son of man" with five letters has forty-one anagrams, a modest increase. But "Ezra," the four-letter name we shall work with, produces 2,443 anagrams. Moving from four Hebrew letters to three, the increase in number of anagrams is substantial. The three-letter name "Shaphan" brings almost thirty-two thousand anagrams to Scripture.

For now, we shall stick to the simplest form of this art, the four-letter BA. Although Scripture contains over twenty-four hundred "Ezra" BAs, about thirty specific stems account for close to two-thirds of that total. In biblical times, a literate child who had been taught athbash could easily spot a majority of the "Ezra" BAs. "Aaron," by far the leading Ezra word, has over 350 occurrences. One of the Ezra athbash variations is הנאר (see table 1.2), which, with modest scrambling, becomes "Aaron," אהרן. Next in frequency comes "arise," ויקם, a common narrative device, as in, "When Lot saw them, he rose to meet them" (Gen 19:1). BAs formed by this word occur nearly three hundred times. Numbers 30, for example, contains eight of them.

No athbash at all is required for "Eleazar," which makes seventy-seven appearances. It simply adds ל to עזרא, "Ezra," to spell אלעזר, "Eleazar." Numbers 31 has ten Eleazar BAs, every one of which is accompanied by "the priest," a title often associated with Ezra himself. To further dispel coincidence, Eleazar is the son of Aaron, the person whose name is Scripture's leading source of Ezra BAs. Other proper names also contribute. "Jehoiakim," spelled יהויקים, contains the Ezra athbash וקים, while "Jezreel," יזרעאל, has the four actual letters of "Ezra" within it. In Scripture as a whole, "Jehoiakim" has thirty-six BAs and "Jezreel" forty. "Berechiah," "Ahiezer," "Reubinites," and "Araunah" each have between seven and eleven BA spellings (with all nine Araunah BAs appearing in 2 Sam 24).

The root "first" joins "ark," "bless," "chariot," "cherub," "number," "see," and "sin" as the most commonly employed letter groups that carry Ezra BAs. Perhaps the most interesting of nouns is "wheels," אוֹפַנִּים, which houses the Ezra athbash יֽאנף. Seven of these BAs occur in Ezek 1, which contains the famous vision of the four winged creatures. Ezekiel 10 has another seven such BAs, and these are joined by no less than fifteen "cherub"/"cherubim" biblical anagrams within that same chapter. Both הכרוב and הברוכים contain the Ezra athbash רכבה, and each word also spells out "Baruch," which is ברוך. Surely we are permitted to speculate that Ezra and Baruch were subjects (or editors) of the two Ezekiel chapters. Further, since Baruch was, without question, an exilic figure, it is likely that Ezra also lived during the Exile.

Biblical anagrams are amenable to statistical analysis. What, for example, is the probability that twenty-five Ezra BAs occur by coincidence in Ezek 10?[1] Knowing the number of Ezra BAs and words in Scripture, as well as the number of words in the chapter, the computation is easily made. The result is essentially zero.[2] That is, the probability of coincidentally finding twenty-five Ezra BAs in Ezek 10 is expressed as a decimal followed by forty-two zeros.

The foregoing Ezra illustrations showed that the anagram technique was sophisticated and well developed. Perhaps applying it should be a requisite for modern biblical scholarship. The characteristics of BAs are listed below.

- They can be derived using computer search programs.[3]
- They are easily deciphered.
- They are amenable to statistical analysis.

---

1. Two other spellings formed from "wheels" and "cherubim" bring the total of Ezra BAs in Ezek 10 to twenty-five.

2. The chi-square proportions are 25 / 2,419 and 310 / 304,591. $P = 4.22 \times 10^{-43}$. The first proportion consists of Ezra BAs in Ezek 10 and in the remainder of Scripture, while the second has text words in the same categories.

3. The twenty-four ways to spell a four-letter word (abcd, abdc, acbd . . . bacd, etc.) can be assembled with a single search using BibleWorks. After running the search, send results to a word processing file and then cancel verses that contain duplicate anagrams in the same text word. Repeat these steps for each of the other athbash versions.

The Shaphan Group

- They employ athbash, which adds vocabulary options and shields information from outside view.
- They enhance the meaning of biblical texts.
- They can accommodate multiple names within single text words.
- They encompass all of Scripture.

This chapter works with BAs of only a dozen of some thirteen hundred Hebrew personal names. Once BAs are established for Scripture's full slate of names, who knows what riches will shine through? Biblical anagrams are capable of sparking a scholarly awakening in the study of the Hebrew Bible.

Ezra the P-Source Author

The Priestly Source is aptly named. One of five principal sources of the opening books of the Bible, the Priestly (or P) Source author argues unabashedly for the status and causes of the Aaronite branch of Israel's priesthood. According to the P Source, in ancient times Aaron, the brother of Moses and grandson of Levi, became the first chief priest. He alone was allowed once a year to enter the holy of holies, the inner sanctuary of the tabernacle, to make atonement for the sins of Israel. Other priestly factions, Zadokites and Levites, were subordinated to and served Aaron and his descendants. The task of distinguishing between holy and common, and between clean and unclean, fell upon Aaron. The P material describes at length the priestly functions of the Aaronites, including sacrifice, ordination, sobriety, teaching, treating, and curing. In P's writings, the tabernacle (a tent-sanctuary) is the locus of priestly activities, and neither Solomon's temple nor its post-exilic successor is ever mentioned.

An intriguing problem with all of this is that scholars have been unable to substantiate any official Aaronite priesthood in the pre-Exilic period.[4] Despite the glorification in the Priestly Source writings of Moses' brother Aaron, non-P Source texts barely mention Aaron, much less Aaron as a priest. Surprisingly, Ezekiel, who prophesied from Babylon during the Exile, knew only of Zadokite priests supported by Levites. Control of the priesthood seems to have passed from Zadokite-Levite

---

4. Blenkinsopp, "Assessment of Priestly Material," 502.

hands during the monarchy to Aaronite domination after the Exile. Who and what could have accomplished a thing of this tectonic magnitude?

We think that it happened this way. An athbash BA of Ezra contains the same letters as אהרן, "Aaron." Someone—probably Ezra himself—used a BA to forge an Aaron-Ezra connection, a connection that had escaped notice until this writer rediscovered the ancient athbash technique. The Aaron of Scripture was Moses' brother—his *elder* brother, the first high priest, the one from whom all lawful priests were to descend.[5] The Ezra of Judah was a son of the high priest whom Nebuchadnezzar executed at Riblah. However, it was Ezra's brother Jozadak who seems to have succeeded the father as high priest, though Jozadak was exiled (1 Chr 6:15) while Ezra probably remained in Judah. Moreover, at the start of the Exile, Babylon demolished Solomon's temple, depriving Judah's high priest of a place to serve. It could well be that "Aaron" was Ezra's invention, a fabrication designed to clothe the Aaronites with priestly authority at the expense of the exiled Zadokite-Levite faction. If so, this solves a previously intractable mystery.

Like many others, for a number of years I have sought to identify the P Source. In making this search, I had the advantage of understanding coding, athbash, and BAs. One day, while counting out BAs for exilic leaders against Pentateuch chapters, I noticed that the totals for "Ezra" seemed exceptionally high for the books of Exodus and Numbers. Curious, I sought closer definition of the parts of Scripture that experts attributed to P.

Text penned by the P Source is said to be easily recognizable—if only because it is so uninspired. That author and his school loved lists, trite formulas, and pedantic descriptions. Allowing for differing scholarly insights, there is general agreement about the boundaries of P-Source text. Richard Elliott Friedman has done us the service of pulling together side-by-side the views of three experts.[6] The foremost of these is Martin Noth, who drew his conclusions about the P corpus over six decades ago. The two other authorities are Karl Ellinger and Norbert Lohfink.

As a base from which to measure, I made a composite of the three views, including every verse that each expert thought was from P. The list-

---

5. Mauch, "Aaron," 2.

6. The compilation is in Friedman, *Exile*, 87–91. Individual listings are in Noth, *Pentateuchal Traditions*, 17–19; Ellinger, "Sinn und Ursprung," 121–22; and Lohfink, "Die Priesterrschrift," 198.

ing assumed that any verse mentioned was complete rather than partial (as a few were). Differences between the three experts were modest—well below ten percent. The completed list totals 14,834 text words, which is over one thousand verses. Exodus contributed the most P text, Genesis and Numbers ranked second and third, and Leviticus was a distant fourth. Joshua and Deuteronomy also contained a few verses that at least one expert thought originated with the P Source. This experts' composite of P-Source writings constituted half of the authorship test. The source for the other half originated from Ezra BAs.

There are exactly 2,443 Ezra BAs within Scripture, 273 of which are included within the composite. That composite contains 14,834 Hebrew words; Scripture as a whole has 305,496. After rearranging the data, it requires less than a minute to enter them into one's calculator. The chi-square result is the probability of coincidence of these two independent sets of numbers occurring together. The result is $P = 8.21 \times 10^{-47}$.[7] The probability of finding by coincidence 273 BAs in the experts' P-Source composite is zero.

The author of the P-Source material intentionally employed Ezra BAs, and that makes Ezra a prime candidate for P-Source author. There may be a few others whose BAs will draw as impressive a result. If so, when and if they are found, let them stand alongside Ezra as co-authors. (It will be several years before the technology exists for a comprehensive review of all possible candidates.) For now, however, probability announces that Ezra is a leading member of the long-sought P Source. Roughly, it appears that Ezra had a hand in three-quarters of the verses in the P-Source composite. Genesis holds most of the other three hundred to four hundred verses that experts attribute to P—verses that Ezra did not write.

However, tracking down other P-Source authors may not matter much. Because of the coding and anagram discoveries, we could be at the start of a new phase in scholarly biblical studies. The old source approach should gradually give way to assigning names (and probably dates) to passages. Certainly this will apply to texts written from the late monarchy forward. As to earlier material, we simply do not know yet whether, say, the J Source employed encryption—though this question could well be settled within the next decade.

---

7. The chi-square proportions are 273 / 2,170 and 14,834 / 290,662. $P = 4.96 \times 10^{-47}$. The first proportion consists of Ezra BAs in the experts' P-Source composite and in the rest of Scripture, while the second has the text words in the same categories.

An Exilic Ezra

When did the P Source live? About this, scholars disagree. Julius Wellhausen, who originated the Documentary Hypothesis and the P Source title, thought that the Priestly writer worked early in the Persian period.[8] Jacob Milgrom states that P "was composed not later than the middle of the 8th century."[9] Frank Cross writes that the Priestly work "must have been completed in the sixth century, late in the Exile."[10] Antony Campbell and Mark O'Brien opt for shortly before, during, or soon after the Exile.[11] And Richard E. Friedman leans toward Hezekiah's reign (late eighth century), though that scholar had previously said that there was wide consensus for placing P in the Exile.[12]

Scripture attempts to place a person named Ezra in the Restoration Period, perhaps a century and one-half after the Exile. However, the material in Scripture about Restoration Ezra is disordered, and there is a noticeable lack of interplay between Nehemiah and Ezra.[13] Ezra 7:1 identifies an Ezra of the Restoration as "Ezra son of Seraiah" who lived "in the reign of King Artaxerxes of Persia." But the part about Artaxerxes is incorrect. The chief priest Seraiah died at Nebuchadnezzar's hand at the start of the Exile. A different genealogy of high priests in Chronicles reads, "Azariah begot Seraiah, Seraiah begot Jehozadak [Jozadak]; and Jehozadak went into exile . . ." (1 Chr 6:14–15). Thus Seraiah fathered both Ezra and Jehozadak. Presumably, Jehozadak (also spelled Jozadak) was the older son and succeeded to the chief priesthood after Nebuchadnezzar slew the father. The *IDB* wrote, "Ezra also claims descent from Seraiah . . . and thus it can be assumed that Ezra went into exile with his brother Jehozadak. However, Jehozadak was evidently Seraiah's first-born son."[14] (As we shall come to understand, the matter of which brother should have inherited the priestly title became a matter of bitter contention.) Some even think that Ezra was a fiction. The *ABD* states that after G. Garbini's 1986 book, "there was a strong scholarly revival of the opinion that Ezra never

---

8. See Hurowitz, "Priestly Source," 37.
9. Milgrom, "Priestly Source," 459.
10. Cross, *Canaanite Myth*, 325.
11. Campbell and O'Brien, *Sources of Pentateuch*, 21.
12. Friedman, *Who Wrote the Bible?* 213; *Exile*, 116.
13. Ackroyd, *Exile and Restoration*, 191–92.
14. Achtemeier, "Seraiah," 279. Also see Kavanagh, *Exilic Code*, 92–98.

The Shaphan Group

existed."[15] Scripture seems ambivalent about when Ezra lived, and some doubt that he lived at all.

Fortunately, biblical anagrams settle these Ezra questions with overwhelming probabilities. When we use BAs to probe Ezra's relationship with anagrams of other exilic characters, we find surprising things. The five parties tested were Ezra himself, Jacob, Baruch, Cyrus, and Jozadak. Jacob is Second Isaiah's name, Cyrus is the Persian conqueror, and Jozadak is the exiled son of the high priest. Table 2.1 totals the single text words that contain multiple BAs of these five persons. With this approach, probabilities can give us a quick reading on the strength of relationships among the five. Despite differences in total and shared BAs, every one of those relationships approaches zero probability of coincidence. For example, the probability that so many Ezra and Jacob BAs would land on identical text words—592 Ezra BAs and 592 Jacob BAs—is zero. Stated another way, a blindfolded person pulling balls from a large vat has zero chance of having one-fourth of two thousand picks be red balls, given that only one ball of every hundred in the vat is red.[16] In table 2.1 below, "Sign" in the right column stands for "statistically significant."

TABLE 2.1
Multiple BAs in Single Text Words

	BAs	E	J	B	Cy	Sign
Ezra	2,443		592	278	65	All
Jacob	2,238	592		84	26	All
Baruch	2,066	278	84		66	All
Cyrus	999	65	26	66		All
Jozadak	279	76	72	11	23	All

15. North, "Ezra," 727. North cited Garbini, *Storia e ideologia*, 1986.

16. Jacob BAs within Scripture total 2,238, while those of Ezra total 2,443. Also, Scripture contains 305,496 text words. The chi-square proportions are 592 / 1,646 and 1,851 / 301,407. P = 0. The first proportion consists of shared Jacob-Ezra BAs in Scripture over Jacob-only BAs in the rest of Scripture, while the second has the number of text words with Ezra-only BAs over the balance of text words in Scripture that contain no Ezra or Jacob BAs.

Anagrams Uncover Priestly Source

The relationship between Ezra the P Source and Jacob-Second Isaiah was close, so the chances are very good that they collaborated on texts. Moreover, at 592, the sheer quantity of double Ezra-Jacob BAs is large. There are nearly twice as many Ezra-Jacob BAs as the 278 between Ezra and Baruch. Ezra and Jacob almost certainly wrote a lot of Scripture together.

Ezra's total number of multiple BAs is substantially higher than Jacob's and easily exceeds the totals for Baruch and for Jozadak. This fits well with Ezra's reputation among the rabbis as a learned, literary man. Scripture documents that Baruch, who was Jeremiah's right hand, was a skilled scribe, while Jozadak must have been a priest-in-training for some years prior to his father's execution. To be first among three such companions speaks highly for Ezra. Also, excluding Cyrus, note the way that this group spans the later monarchy and the Exile. I myself had previously drawn a firm line between the two periods, and perhaps other analysts have also done so. But two and probably all four of these men could have worked during both the monarchy and the Exile. This knowledge will be useful when considering additional P-Source writers, the identities of psalm and proverbs authors, and whether there were other Dtr contributors.

The figures in table 2.1 tell us something else: Ezra, Jacob, Baruch, and Jozadak were significantly involved with Cyrus the Great. The four probably plotted together to enlist Cyrus to lead a rebellion in Judah. Work published elsewhere suggests that such a thing took place in the later 570s, and that Baruch and perhaps Ezra fought alongside Cyrus.[17]

Table 2.1 covers pairs of anagrams. However, roots of the two text words "elders" and "eastern" contain BAs for four names each. Together, they appear in seven places, which are detailed in the note.[18] In another feat of composition, the author of Esth 9:3 packed four separate athbash spellings of "Ezra" alone into the word והאחשדרפנים, which means

---

17. Kavanagh, *Secrets*, 361–70.

18. Jacob, Ezra, Baruch, and Cyrus have BAs within the single word "elders," והזקנים, in 2 Kgs 6:31, 10:5; 1 Chr 21:16; and Ezra 10:8. The athbash spelling for Jacob is קמיה, for Baruch יוין, for Ezra וקים, and for Cyrus קננז. The word "eastern," הקדמוני, appears in Ezek 10:19 and 11:1 and in Zech 14:8. The athbash spellings for Jacob, Baruch, and Ezra are the same as those above. The athbash version of Cyrus is נקהד.

The Shaphan Group

"and the satraps."[19] And the Hebrew word for "numbered," לופקדיהם, actually accommodates five BAs, two of which are Ezra variants.[20]

"Jacob" is the name of the previously unknown prophet of the Exile whom we call Second Isaiah. A lengthy chapter devoted to this elsewhere spares readers a full recounting.[21] For our purposes, it will suffice to give a brief summary of why we can safely conclude that Jacob was indeed Second Isaiah's name.

- Vocabulary from a strong Word Link connects the Isa 49 description of Jacob's naming with his birth story in Genesis, and the two accounts fit well together.
- Rabbinic tradition and significant Jacob coding in Second Isaiah chapters also support the Jacob finding.
- The prophet's frequent use in Isa 40–55 of "Jacob" and "Israel" marks these as signatures, termed IDs. "Holy One of Israel" and Jacob-Israel parallels are the most significant IDs.
- IDs and coding establish a significant Jacob presence in Psalms.

While the exilic provenance of "Jacob" has yet to be widely acknowledged, there can be no question about Cyrus the Persian, Jozadak the priest, or Baruch the scribe. These were clearly sixth-century individuals and were well known to Scripture's writers. Probabilities, though both useful and powerful, have not generally been employed in biblical scholarship. Although these Ezra, Jacob, Baruch, Jozadak, and Cyrus combinations speak for themselves, we shall soon introduce scores of examples that also demonstrate the close connection between Ezra the P Source and other leading personages of his time—which was the Exile.

---

19. The four Ezra athbash spellings are הנאר, יאנף, פדמי, and שחפן. That same Esth 9:3 word (והאחשדרפנים) contains BAs of Cyrus, Daniel, messiah, Baruch, and Qohelet.

20. The word occurs in Exod 30:12; Num 3:43, and 26:18, 22, 25, 27, 37, 43, 47. The Cyrus, Jozadak, Jacob, and two Ezra BAs are פלדה, מפהקד, קמיה, פדמי, and וקים, respectively.

21. See Kavanagh, "Second Isaiah's Identity," *Exilic Code*, 62–84. The summary is on 79.

Anagrams Uncover Priestly Source

The Cyrus Catastrophe

Previously we introduced readers to several things that may have seemed novel. These include athbash, coding, and biblical anagrams. Applying these techniques led to discoveries that Ezra is the P Source and that he practiced during the Exile. The next disclosure concerns Cyrus the Great, the Persian who conquered Babylon in 539 BCE and ended the Exile of the Jews. We have outlined elsewhere that a Cyrus-led revolt occurred in Israel in the late 570s, a revolt planned and financed by Jacob, Baruch, and Ezra.[22] That uprising ended in disaster, when Nebuchadnezzar repressed it with enthusiastic help from Judah's neighbors. As one would expect, the taint of treason spread to the exiles in Babylon. A persecution followed and resulted in the execution of Ezekiel, who was the Suffering Servant.[23]

Knowledge about the Cyrus uprising is crucial for understanding the context of the P Source's work. Here, BAs offer clues. In Gen 42–44, Joseph, a power in Pharaoh's court, recognizes his brothers, who have come from Palestine to seek food. There is much talk of spies (מרגלים), and Jacob's brothers unwittingly transport sacks (אמתחת) filled with silver. The Cyrus anagrams גרלם and מתחא lie within these text words, and Gen 42–44 contains a total of twenty-five BAs—far too many to be coincidental.[24] Jacob and Daniel each have a number of BAs and the exiled Jozadak and King Jehoiachin also have a few. Clearly a plot was afoot, and money was changing hands.

Leviticus 25 contains the next episode of the Cyrus-revolt story. With expectations centering upon Cyrus, even before conquest, the Jewish rebels are reserving and dividing property:

> Throughout the land that you hold [Cyrus BA], you shall provide for the redemption of the land. If anyone of your kin falls into difficulty and sells a piece of property [Cyrus BA], then the next of kin shall come and redeem what the relative has sold . . . the Levites shall forever have the right of redemption of the houses in the cities [Cyrus BA] belonging to them . . . the houses in the cities of the Levites are their possession [Cyrus BA] . . . You may keep them as a possession [Cyrus BA] for your children after you . . . (Lev 25:24–25, 32–33, 46)

---

22. Kavanagh, *Exilic Code*, 33–37.
23. Ibid., 107–25.
24. The probability of coincidence is 5.6×10^{-20}.

The Shaphan Group

The liberation of the land seems imminent, and we can date the chapter as not long before 572 BCE. Leviticus 25 is toward the end of the so-called Holiness Code. Though the chapter is priestly literature, it was not the work of Ezra, the P Source. Still, at least the portion after v 24 was written with Cyrus in mind. And though not quoted, the chapter contains a sixth Cyrus BA in the first word of the seventh verse, which suggests that Lev 25 was either edited or entirely composed in the later 570s.

Leviticus 26 stands as a classic example of the assistance that cryptography can bring to interpretation. The chapter has significant "Ezra" coding as well as significant "Ezra" anagrams—an unusual combination. Strikingly, one can draw a before-and-after line between verses 13 and 14 to mark the time of the Cyrus disaster (and neither half speaks well of Ezra). The opening verses caution against graven images and contain two Ezra BAs—תקימו, "set up," in v 1 and ומקדסי, "and my sanctuary," in v 2. Each yields the Ezra BA וקים. So does the final word in v 13—קוממיות, "erect." In between, in verses 3 through 12, there are five Daniel BAs.[25] Also, there appears to be a lengthy insert by Jacob and Ezra about prospering in war and on the land. The insert concludes, "I will look with favor upon you and make you fruitful and multiply you; and I will maintain [Ezra and Jacob BAs] my covenant with you" (Lev 26:9).

Then havoc breaks loose.

> But if you will not obey me . . . and you break my covenant . . . you shall be struck down by your enemies; your foes shall rule over you, and you shall flee though no one pursues you. . . . I will continue to punish you sevenfold for your sins [Cyrus BA]. . . . I will continue to plague you sevenfold for your sins [Cyrus BA]. . . . If in spite of these punishments you . . . continue [Cyrus BA] hostile to me . . . I myself will strike you sevenfold for your sins [Cyrus BA]. . . . If you . . . continue [Cyrus BA] hostile to me, I will continue hostile to you in fury; I in turn will punish you myself sevenfold for your sins [Cyrus BA] . . . I will heap your carcasses [Cyrus BA] on the carcasses of your idols.[26]

---

25. Two of the five Daniel BAs are the word for eunuch-official (*saris*), which I have assumed stands for Daniel. Previous work leads me to believe that "Qoheleth," preacher, might also be a term for Daniel. Lev 26:13–15 contain pairs of Daniel, *saris*, and Qoheleth BAs.

26. Lev 26:14–15, 17–18, 21, 23–24, 27–29.

The Holiness-Code author saw not only military defeat from the sinful alliance with Cyrus but also apostasy and idol worship. The defeat must have been crushing because exile is clearly stated: "The land shall enjoy its sabbath years as long as it lies desolate, while you are in the land of your enemies" (Lev 26:34). A few words later, we have, "And those of you who survive [Ezra and Jacob BAs] will languish in the land of their enemies because of their iniquities [Ezra BA]; also . . . the iniquities [Ezra BA] of their ancestors" (26:39). Note the clever jab at the ancestor whom Ezra claimed; surely Aaron was intended. One suspects that the author was a Zadokite priest writing from Babylonia.[27]

In the next section of Lev 26, Jacob replies, writing about God's mercy. In their enemies' land, "if then their uncircumcised heart is humbled and they make amends for their iniquity, then will I remember my covenant with Jacob." Further along, "when they are in the land of their enemies, I will not spurn them [Cyrus BA], or abhor them so as to destroy them utterly and break [Daniel BA] my covenant with them; for I am the LORD their God."[28]

The last word in this extraordinary chapter belongs to Jacob. He closes Lev 26 and the rest of the Holiness Code with: "These are the statutes [Jacob BA] and ordinances and laws that the LORD established between himself and the people of Israel on Mount Sinai through Moses" (Lev 26:46).

The chapter is like a stratified cliff thrust up by a sudden movement of the earth. Its earliest stratum contains Ezra, Jacob, and Daniel BAs, and speaks of allocating the land and prospering on it. The next layer violently condemns Cyrus and those who have sinned with him, using BAs to threaten Jacob and Ezra. The theme that predominates is "I will strike you sevenfold for your sins [Cyrus BA]."

In the chapter's third layer, Jacob announces that the Lord will yet renew His covenant with the land and with His penitent people.

---

27. There are repeated references to "the land of their enemies." While whomever the Israelites fought were acting in the interests of Babylon, the soldiers they faced were unlikely to have been from Babylon, which did not garrison the provinces it conquered. Instead, "the land of their enemies" was more likely to have been Moab, Syria, Ammon, Midian, or another neighboring country.

28. Lev 26:41–42, 44.

The Shaphan Group

The fourth stratum of Lev 26 is the finale—the concluding verse that completes the Holiness Code. One would expect this to have come from a Zadokite, but Jacob has used a BA to sign it himself.

Apparently the rebellion that ended so miserably also had its high point, which we can detect through Cyrus BAs in a Genesis chapter. "King Melchizedek [Cyrus BA] of Salem brought out bread and wine; he was priest of God Most High. He blessed him [Baruch and Ezra BAs] and said, 'Blessed [Baruch BA] be Abram . . . and blessed [Baruch BA] be God Most High, who has delivered your enemies into your hand!' And Abram gave him one tenth of everything. Then the king of Sodom said to Abram, 'Give me the persons, but take the goods [Cyrus BA] for yourself'" (Gen 14:18–21).[29]

Weighing the anagram evidence, it appears that Melchizedek was at once Cyrus and the high priest of Salem, which would have been Jerusalem. The fact that Abram paid him a tithe, according to Michael Astour, "legitimizes the aspirations of the high priests of Jerusalem," and also "proclaimed the ideal of theocracy in the Priestly Code."[30] Notably, Ezra had a BA in the passage. Since Melchizedek had been transformed from a covenant-breaking mercenary to a chief-priest and a king of righteousness, the Genesis passage may be post-exilic. However, the exilic characters—Cyrus, Baruch, and Ezra—ring true and so does the split of booty. Apparently, the victors were members of a coalition that included Sodom (probably Edom). Perhaps Cyrus and his Judahites even captured Jerusalem. (Evidence later in this book indicates that they did.) At a minimum, the Cyrus-led forces counted some victories before suffering their desolating defeat.

Turning from Gen 14 to Ezek 34, BAs tell us that Cyrus escaped from Canaan to fight again. In verses 18 and 19, Ezekiel packs eight Cyrus anagrams into a vivid word picture of animals befouling Israel's pasture. Biblical anagrams for Ezra, Baruch, and Jacob are in nearby verses. This concentration of Cyrus BAs in Ezekiel is without parallel in Scripture. Here is the passage:

---

29. "Melchizedek" is formed from two Hebrew words and requires letters from both to construct a BA for "Cyrus." Because the MT uses a *maqqeph* to join ומלכי and צדק, and because the passage contains an additional Cyrus BA, I have assumed that the two words in Gen 14:18 also form a BA.

30. Astour, "Melchizedek," 684.

Anagrams Uncover Priestly Source

Is it not enough for you to feed on the good pasture, but you must tread down with your feet [two Cyrus BAs] the rest of your pasture? When you drink of clear water, must you foul the rest with your feet [two Cyrus BAs]? And must my sheep eat what you have trodden with your feet [two Cyrus BAs], and drink what you have fouled with your feet [two Cyrus BAs]?[31]

Yet other lines from a psalm sum up what the Jewish survivors thought of Cyrus. It is a telling characterization of a great but ruthless man. "My companion stretched out his hand against his friends, he violated his covenant. His speech was smoother than butter [Cyrus BA], yet war was in his heart; his words were softer than oil, yet they were drawn swords" (Ps 55:21-22 RSV [Heb 22-23]).

Biblical anagrams tell us that Jacob, Baruch, and Ezra in Israel and Daniel, Jozadak, and King Jehoiachin in Babylon were deeply involved in the Cyrus plot. Ezekiel, who opposed the scheme, lost his life because of it. The prophet's resistance under torture, however, bought freedom for Daniel and Jehoiachin. Although Jehoiachin escaped death immediately after the uprising, the Babylonians killed him as a substitute king in 561 BCE. Extensive work with Word Links (in another volume) indicates that Baruch was captured in the Cyrus debacle and suffered badly before being ransomed.[32] While Ezra might also have been taken and held for ransom,[33] the sheer volume of his post-revolt priestly writing argues against this.

Sinful Cyrus, Sinful Ezra

The word חטאת, meaning "sin," appears often in Scripture in various forms. Fully twenty-eight of its variations hold within a single text word athbash BAs of מחטו (Ezra) and of מחתא (Cyrus).[34] That is, biblical readers were repeatedly reminded that the redoubtable Ezra was sinfully

---

31. In each of four cases, Ezekiel fashions two Cyrus BAs—גרלם and רגבי—from רגליכם, "your feet." See Kavanagh, *Exilic Code*, 33-34 for further discussion of the Cyrus revolt.

32. Kavanagh, *Secrets*, 283-91.

33. Ibid., 286.

34. Gen 18:20, 50:17; Lev 4:26, 5:6, 19:22; Num 15:25; Deut 20:18; Josh 24:19; 1 Kgs 8:35; 2 Kgs 13:6, 15:9 and 24, 21:16; Neh 4:5 [Heb 3:37]; Ps 51:3 [Heb 52:4]; Isa 3:9, 59:2; Jer 5:25, 16:18, 18:23, 31:34, 36:3; Ezek 21:24 [Heb 21:29], 33:14; Hos 8:13; 9:9 and 10; Mic 7:19.

The Shaphan Group

involved with Cyrus the Persian. These sin BAs account for half of all the Ezra-Cyrus connections within a single text word, and we know already that those connections were intentionally made (see table 2.1). A majority of the combinations criticized Ezra, though others attempted to pardon the man who aspired to be Israel's high priest. One-third of Scripture's books carry this double BA, which is interesting in itself. This indicates that the controversy was widely fought over an extended period of time. The Ezra-Cyrus-sin words even appear in Neh 3, which must have been written a good century after the Cyrus rebellion.

Two Ezra-Cyrus passages follow. "Then the LORD said, 'How great is the outcry against Sodom and Gomorrah and how very grave their sin [Cyrus and Ezra BAs]!'" (Gen 18:20) and "The look on their faces bears witness against them; they proclaim their sin [Cyrus and Ezra BAs] like Sodom, they do not hide it. Woe to them!" (Isa 3:9). These passages associate Ezra with the depravity of that ancient city.

Four other BAs came from Second Kings, which shows that that book was still open after the late 570s. "Nevertheless they did not depart from the sins of the house of Jeroboam, which he caused Israel to sin [Cyrus and Ezra BAs]"; "He did what was evil in the sight of the LORD, *as his ancestors had done* [emphasis added]. He did not depart from the sins of Jeroboam son of Nebat, which he caused Israel to sin [Cyrus and Ezra BAs]"; and again, "He did not turn away from the sins of Jeroboam son of Nebat, which he caused Israel to sin [Cyrus and Ezra BAs]" (2 Kgs 13:6; 15:9, 24). And what was the sin of Jeroboam? He built calves of gold at Dan and Bethel. The writer could be reminding readers that Ezra had ties to Bethel where Aaron-Ezra might also have fashioned a golden calf. In addition, there is the phrase "as his ancestors had done." Surely the Second Kings author inserted those words to recall Aaron's sacrilege.

The other Second Kings biblical anagram is in this verse, "Manasseh shed very much innocent blood, until he had filled Jerusalem from one end to another, besides the sin [Cyrus and Ezra BAs] that he caused Judah to sin . . ." (2 Kgs 21:16). If the decisive battle of the Cyrus revolt took place amidst the capitol's ruins, then the words "shed very much innocent blood, until he had filled Jerusalem from one end to another . . ." take on a more contemporary meaning. Moreover, earlier in that chapter, the author had written that King Manasseh had "erected [Ezra BA] altars for Baal" (2 Kgs 21:3).[35] From Deuteronomy comes: ". . . so that they may

35. The list of Manasseh's offenses against the Lord also concealed three Daniel BAs.

not teach you to do all the abhorrent things that they do for their gods, and you thus sin [Cyrus and Ezra BAs] against the Lord your God" (Deut 20:18).

Jeremiah also weighed in against the Ezra and Cyrus, and in turn Jacob and Jehoiachin felt his wrath. "Your iniquities [Jehoiachin BA] have turned these away, and your sins [Cyrus and Ezra BAs] have deprived you of good"; "I will doubly [Jacob and Ezra BAs] repay their iniquity and their sin [Cyrus and Ezra BAs], because they have polluted my land with the carcasses of their detestable [Ezra and *two* Jacob BAs] idols"; and "do not blot out their sin [Cyrus and Ezra BAs] from your sight . . . deal with them while you are angry" (Jer 5:25; 16:18; 18:23). Jeremiah would have made these pronouncements about 573 BCE, if our dating of the uprising is correct. How old would the prophet have been at that time? One expert thinks that Jeremiah was born about 640.[36] That would put him in his late sixties when the fighting in Israel ended and Cyrus had fled. This is old but certainly not too old. Clearly, the elderly prophet had retained his verve and animus.

Ezekiel also had a strong opinion. He wrote, "Because you have brought your guilt to remembrance, in that your transgressions [Jehoiachin BA] are uncovered, so that in all your deeds your sins [Cyrus and Ezra BAs] appear—because you have come to remembrance, you shall be taken in hand" (Ezek 21:24). Ezekiel may still have been at liberty in Babylon when he wrote this, but Jehoiachin probably was not. The exiled king would have been arrested ("taken in hand") and put to torture in order to uncover his role in the Cyrus plot.

Next, an as yet unidentified person wrote in Josh 24:19: "'You cannot serve the LORD, for he is a holy God. He is a jealous God; he will not forgive your transgressions [Jehoiachin BA] or your sins [Cyrus and Ezra BAs].'"[37] Further, a writer in Hosea added Daniel to the list: "Though they offer choice sacrifices [Jehoiachin BA], though they eat [Daniel BA] flesh, the Lord does not accept them. Now he will remember their iniquity, and punish their sins [Cyrus and Ezra BAs]; they shall return to Egypt."[38] Also, "They have deeply [Ezra BA] corrupted themselves as in the days of Gibeah; he will remember their iniquity, he will punish their sins [Cyrus

---

36. Lundbom, "Jeremiah," 686.

37. The author of Josh 24:19 probably was Asaiah, servant of the king under Josiah (2 Kgs 22:12).

38. Here the author uses a saris BA in place of one for Daniel.

and Ezra BAs]" (Hos 8:13, 9:9). "Gibeah" probably refers to the shame brought upon Israel by the rape and murder of the Levite's concubine (Judg 20).

Later sources show that the animosity continued: "Do not cover their guilt, and do not let their sin [Cyrus and Ezra BAs] be blotted out from your sight; for they have hurled insults in the face of the builders" (Neh 4:5 [Heb. 3:37]). "Hurled insults in the face of the builders"—the factionalism was impeding restoration work on Jerusalem's wall more than one hundred years later! Another text shows how this schism persisted. Isaiah 59:2 says, "Your iniquities [Jehoiachin BA] have been barriers between you and your God, and your sins [Cyrus, Daniel, and Ezra BAs] have hidden his face from you so that he does not hear."

Penitent Ezra

In the face of these critics, Ezra or his colleagues showed contrition. Genesis 50:17 pleaded, "'Say to Joseph: I beg you, forgive the crime of your brothers and the wrong [Cyrus and Ezra BAs] they did in harming you.' 'Now therefore please forgive the crime of the servants of the God of your father.' Joseph wept when they spoke to him."

Often, the request was phrased in priestly terms: "The priest shall make atonement for all the congregation of the Israelites, and they shall be forgiven; it was unintentional, and they have brought their . . . sin offering [Cyrus and Ezra BAs] before the LORD, for their error" (Num 15:25). Three Leviticus texts were similar: "The priest shall make atonement on his behalf for his sin [Cyrus and Ezra BAs], and he shall be forgiven"; "And you shall bring to the LORD . . . a sheep or a goat, as a sin offering; and the priest shall make atonement on your behalf for your sin [Cyrus and Ezra BAs]"; and "The priest shall make atonement for him with the ram of guilt offering . . . for his sin that he committed, and the sin [Cyrus and Ezra BAs] he committed shall be forgiven him" (Lev 4:26, 5:6, 19:22). Although these passages pleaded for Ezra, not one made the list of P-Source texts.

Perhaps because of these supplications, the prophets begin to bend. Jeremiah says, "When the house of Judah hears of all the disasters that I intend to do to them, all of them may turn from their evil ways, so that I may forgive their iniquity and their sin [Cyrus and Ezra BAs]" (Jer 36:3). Ezekiel writes, "Again, though I say to the wicked, 'You shall surely die,' yet if they turn from their sin [Cyrus and Ezra BAs] and do what is lawful and right . . ." (Ezek 33:14). Ezekiel had but a narrow window in which to write this—the time between the Cyrus uprising and his own execution as the Suffering Servant. If we assigned 570 BCE to this text, we would not be far astray. Another Cyrus-Ezra BA appears in the book of Jeremiah, although the author is other than the prophet—perhaps Ezra's companion Jacob. Jeremiah 31:34 says, "No longer shall they teach one another, or say to each other, 'Know the LORD,' for they shall all know me, from the least of them to the greatest, says the LORD; for I will forgive their iniquity, and remember their sin [Cyrus and Ezra BAs] no more." The prophet Jacob was a major source for the Book of Comfort, which includes at least Jer 30–31 and probably several chapters beyond.[39]

The Ezra ally who revised the book of Micah sympathetically writes, "He will again have compassion upon us; he will tread our iniquities under foot. You will cast all our sins [Cyrus and Ezra BAs] into the depths of the sea" (Mic 7:19). Solomon's long prayer in 1 Kgs 8 suggests that grudging forgiveness could follow repentance. When "they pray toward this place, confess your name, and turn from their sin [Cyrus and Ezra BAs], because you punish them . . ." (1 Kgs 8:35). And finally, Psalm 51, the great penitential prayer, makes Ezra's offense its centerpiece: "Wash me thoroughly from my iniquity, and cleanse me from my sin [Cyrus and Ezra BAs]" (Ps 51:2 [Heb. 51:3]).

This great sin, this grave offense that destroyed so much and killed so many—the Cyrus uprising of the 570s—has been a secret for two thousand years, except perhaps to a diminishing number of Jews who for a time still understood how to apply athbash and anagrams to Scripture. But guessing when these secrets were lost is not this chapter's task. Instead, it is to focus upon what the new techniques can reveal about the life and times of the P Source. To begin, we have learned that a principal author of the P writings was Ezra. BAs yoked to probability disclose this. Probability also makes it certain that Ezra, Jacob, Cyrus, and Baruch were contemporaries, and hence that the P Source wrote during the sixth-century Exile. Others have also reached this conclusion, and this author's finding confirms theirs.

Finally, we hope that readers of these few pages take note of the power that anagrams confer upon biblical commentators.

---

39. See Kavanagh, *Exilic Code*, 77–78, for Jacob's influence; see Lundbom, "Jeremiah," 714–15, for the scope of the Book of Comfort.

The Shaphan Group

The Date of the P Source Complete

When during the Exile did Ezra write? The twenty-eight Cyrus-Ezra-sin texts reviewed in this chapter allow us to offer a conclusion. Assume that an uprising date in the late 570s has merit. We know that not one of those sin verses falls within the 1,135 verses of the experts' composite P-Source text. True, Ezra's colleagues would never have initiated the double-BA word for sin. However, they would have been forced to use החטאת when responding to those who pilloried Ezra for his role in the failed revolt. This author's conclusion is that the P-Source composite must have been written prior to the revolt's conclusion, which was in the late 570s.

To check this, we also examined the number of "Cyrus" BAs (of which the Cyrus-Ezra-sin BAs are but one type) in the P-Source composite text. While the total was within normally expected bounds, nearly twenty Cyrus BAs showed that the plot was under way, that Cyrus had been recruited, and even that an army had been on the move when Ezra had been completing his P-Source text.[40] Things seem to have begun in the area around Haran in northern Mesopotamia. "Abram took his wife Sarai and his brother's son Lot, and all the possessions [Cyrus BA] that they had gathered [Cyrus BA], and the persons whom they had acquired in Haran; and they set forth to go to the land of Canaan" (Gen 12:5).

Naturally, food, clothing, and pay were problems. These passages pertain to provisioning: "... the land could not support both of them living together; for their possessions [Cyrus BA] were so great that they could not live together"; "he drove away all his livestock, all the property [Cyrus BA] that he had gained, the livestock in his possession [Baruch BA] that he had acquired in Paddan-aram, to go to . . . the land of Canaan"; and "This is how you shall eat it: your loins girded, your sandals on your feet [two Cyrus BAs], and your staff in your hand; and you shall eat it hurriedly" (Gen 13:6; 31:18; Exod 12:18).[41] And further, "They also took their livestock [Jacob BA] and the goods [Cyrus BA] that they had acquired

---

40. Thirty Cyrus-BA verses are within the experts' composite of the P Source, which has 1,135 verses. This has a probability of coincidental occurrence of .014. Although this figure appears favorably small, it does not compare well with other outcomes in this chapter. The cutoff figure that this book regularly uses is .001.

41. Ezekiel uses "feet" with its double Cyrus BAs four times in Ezek 34:18–19. He probably was echoing the Exod 12:18 passage by Ezra.

Anagrams Uncover Priestly Source

[Cyrus BA] in the land of Canaan, and they came into Egypt, Jacob and all his offspring with him" (Gen 46:6).

Money is disbursed: "You shall make around it a rim a handbreadth wide, and a molding [Cyrus BA] of gold around the rim" (Exod 25:25). Exodus 37:12 uses the same phrase. And soldiers are clothed: "Then you shall bring his sons, and put [Cyrus BA] tunics on them" (Exod 29:8).

A substantial army was on the march: ". . . on this very day I brought your companies [Cyrus BA] out of the land of Egypt" (Exod 12:17). The word "companies" means armies or hosts. As to size, "The total enrollment . . . counting [Ezra, Jacob, Cyrus BAs] the number of names, was twenty-two thousand two hundred seventy-three" (Num 3:43). In two passages, Ezra linked the promise of Canaan to the Cyrus venture: "I will give to you, and to your offspring after you, the land where you are now an alien [Cyrus BA], all the land of Canaan, for a perpetual holding" (Gen 17:8). Genesis 28:4 is similar.

Governance apparently was to fall to some combination of high priest, Baruch, and elders—"On the eighth day Moses summoned Aaron [Ezra BA] and his sons and the elders [Baruch and Cyrus BAs] of Israel" (Lev 9:1). Ezra may have arranged a transfer of priestly authority to Eleazar his son. God directed, "'Strip Aaron [Ezra BA] of his vestments, and put them on [Cyrus BA] his son Eleazar [Ezra BA]. But Aaron [Ezra BA] shall be gathered to his people, and shall die there'" (Num 20:26).[42] The reason that God gave for preventing Aaron from entering the Promised Land was a dispute at Meribah. Scholars are still seeking to understand this. It may help to know that whatever the dispute, Cyrus was involved. However, this small sample of Cyrus BAs is insufficient to explain the matter.

Who would expect such a ramshackle assemblage to run smoothly? Verses penned by the P Source that have Cyrus BAs within them contain accounts of a sin offering, murmurings against the Lord, and a desire by many to return to "Egypt" from the wilderness of Zin (Lev 19:5; Num 14:29, 27:14; Exod 16:30). This note lists the thirty P-Source verses that contain Cyrus BAs.[43] (A majority of them have previously been cited in

---

42. Biblical anagrams shed a little light on the transfer of priestly authority from Aaron to Eleazar. Both names conceal the same Ezra BA, so perhaps in actuality no transfer took place at Mt. Hor.

43. The following P-Source verses contain Cyrus BAs: Gen 8:19; 10:22; 11:12; 12:5 (2); 13:6; 17:8; 28:4; 31:18; 46:6 (2); Exod 7:28; 12:11 (2), 17; 16:3; 25:25; 29:8, 20; 37:12;

The Shaphan Group

this chapter.) The citations show the plentitude of difficulties in bringing a mercenary-led army of volunteers from the Haran area toward Canaan, and of augmenting these forces with Jews from Egypt. But one thing is clear: not one of the thousand-plus verses in the experts' P-Source consensus speaks of a contrite high priest seeking forgiveness from his fellow Israelites.[44] Though Ezra's P-Source narrative clearly indicates that a military campaign is under way, those writings do not relate the somber conclusion.

In chapter 3, we shall meet Jozadak, Ezra's brother, and learn how their rivalry has left its mark upon Scripture.

38:3; Lev 8:24; 9:1, 15; Num 3:43; 4:14, 29 (2); 20:26; 27:14.

44. There is a possible exception. Lev 9:15, which includes BAs for Cyrus and Jacob, is a sin offering made for the people, so it does not seem to ask for forgiveness for the failure of the entire enterprise.

3

Ezra and Jozadak BAs Sketch Exile's History

Rivalry of Brothers: Ezra Anagrams

Nebuchadnezzar executed Judah's high priest after Jerusalem's fall in 586 BCE. The priest had fathered two sons, Ezra and Jozadak, and though the Babylonians killed many of Judah's leading citizens, the two brothers survived. Scripture says that Jozadak was exiled to Babylon (1 Chr 6:15), while biblical anagrams (BAs) help to clarify Ezra's fate. The final words of Jer 40:6 speak of "the people who were left [הנשארים] in the land" with Gedaliah, the newly appointed governor of Judah. The word הנשארים contains the Ezra BA הנזרא. The parallel verse in 2 Kgs 25:22 with nearly the same spelling has an identical BA, while another Ezra anagram (ויקם in 25:26) reports that Ezra was among those who fled to Egypt after Gedaliah's assassination. These make clear that Ezra remained in the west while others, including his brother Jozadak, went into exile in Babylon.

A list of high priests in Solomon's temple says that Seraiah fathered Jozadak. It then concludes with these words: "Jehozadak went into exile when the LORD sent Judah and Jerusalem into exile by the hand of Nebuchadnezzar" (1 Chr 6:15 [Heb 5:41]). The post-exilic book of Haggai names Joshua "son of Jehozadak, the high priest" no less than five times (Hag 1:1, 12, 14; 2:2, 4). If a son of Jozadak in turn became high priest, then probably Jehozadak himself became his father's successor. The implication is that Jozadak was the elder brother, and first in line of succession. Except that he was not. Ezra was older and held the birthright to the high priesthood—a condition that was to become the subject of considerable Scripture.

We know that Ezra had seniority because opponents played upon it when they attacked him with BAs. For instance, Jehoram "was the firstborn [Ezra BA]. When he had ascended to the throne . . . he put all his brothers to the sword" (2 Chr 21:3–4). Genesis 19 adds incest to murder with the account of the drunken Lot impregnating his daughters. Verses 31–37 feature four Ezra-firstborn anagrams that explain the story. In a different tale, Laban (Jacob's prospective father-in-law), referring to daughters given in marriage, states, "'This is not done in our country—giving the younger before the firstborn [Ezra BA]'" (Gen 29:26).

The word for firstborn requires that a ה be added before it can become an Ezra BA. The critics knew that distinction well, as this example shows: "The sons of Reuben the firstborn [בכור] of Israel. (He was the firstborn [Ezra BA, הבכור] but, because he defiled his father's bed, his birthright was given to the sons of Joseph son of Israel, so that he is not enrolled in the genealogy according to the birthright . . ." (1 Chr 5:1). By adding a single letter, the Chronicles author (a) identified Ezra as firstborn, (b) shamed him, and (c) explained why his name was omitted from the list of high priests at the end of 1 Chr 5. Insults continued. "Cain rose up [Ezra BA] against his brother Abel, and killed him" (Gen 4:8). Cain was older. Also, the Lord "struck Egypt through their firstborn [Ezra BA]" (Ps 136:10).

A passage containing four Ezra anagrams relates how Jacob stole his brother's birthright. Offering stew to a hungry Esau, Jacob insists, "'First sell me your birthright.' Esau said, 'I am about to die; of what use is a birthright [Ezra BA] to me?' Jacob said, 'Swear to me first.' So he swore to him, and sold his birthright to Jacob. Then Jacob gave Esau bread and lentil stew, and he ate and drank, and rose [Ezra BA] and went his way. Thus Esau despised his birthright [Ezra BA]" (Gen 25:31–34). In this story, the author discredits both of the brothers—the heedless Esau for despising his birthright and the sharp-dealing Jacob for gaining it by deceit. And later, Jacob stole more than Esau's birthright. Using subterfuge, Jacob also secured for himself their father's blessing, which had been intended for his brother. After Esau learned of it, "with an exceedingly great and bitter cry" he lamented that Jacob "has supplanted me these two times. He took away my birthright; and look, now he has taken away my blessing [Ezra BA]" (Gen 27:34, 36). Here, Jacob and perhaps Ezra also are dishonored. (Remember that Jacob and Ezra were compatriots.)

Finally, a Genesis author repeats the same motif, except that this time it is Jacob the grandfather who bestows Manasseh's blessing upon the younger grandson Ephraim. Jacob's son Joseph protests, "Not so, my father! Since this one is the firstborn [Ezra BA], put your right hand on his head" (Gen 48:18), which Jacob refused to do. So once again, Ezra was the loser.

Untangling these conflicts seems as formidable a task as explaining alliances during the War of the Roses. Examining the Ezra-BA cases one at a time, however, shows the pattern:

- Firstborn Jehoram kills brothers—Ezra discredited
- Firstborn daughter seduces Lot—Ezra discredited
- Firstborn daughter of Laban has precedence—Ezra discredited
- Firstborn Reuben defiles father's bed—Ezra discredited
- Firstborn Cain kills Abel—Ezra discredited
- Firstborn Esau sells birthright to Jacob—Ezra and Jacob discredited
- Jacob steals blessing from firstborn Esau—Jacob and probably Ezra discredited
- Jacob redirects blessing from firstborn Manasseh—Ezra and Jacob discredited

The Jehoram, Lot, Laban, Reuben, and Cain passages all use BAs to disparage Ezra, the firstborn. The three Jacob-Saga stories were designed to undermine the close working relationship between Ezra the P Source and Jacob the prophet. The implied meaning of the anagram placement is that Jacob was usurping Ezra's priestly functions, a charge that would only have been made after the Exile commenced. Likewise, all the passages stress that Ezra was the elder brother, a matter that assumed importance only after Jozadak's deportation. Given these things, we can assume that these texts originated in the early years of the Exile. This is especially interesting for the passages from the Jacob Saga. (In this writer's opinion, only one of the dozen Genesis chapters that make up this collection originated with the prophet Jacob.¹) The conclusion is that the talented (and still unknown) author of the Jacob Saga was active during the early Exile and was at least mildly hostile to Ezra and to Jacob.

A final passage might clarify this matter of succession. The text of Deut 21:15–17 contains four Ezra BAs formed from "firstborn," so there is no doubt that they apply to the Ezra-Jozadak situation. In addition, consecutive encodings of "Ezra" and his father "Seraiah" dot the Hebrew text.² The passage poses the problem of a man who has two wives and favors one woman over the other. The disliked wife bears a son first and afterwards the favored wife also produces a male child. According to a biblical anagram, Ezra is the child of the less-favored wife, which makes him the older one—"the firstborn [Ezra BA] being the son of the one who is disliked." The husband—who would be Seraiah the high priest—"must acknowledge as firstborn [Ezra BA] the son of the one who is disliked, giving him a double portion of all that he has; since he is the first issue of his virility, the right of the firstborn [Ezra BA] is his."

The verses that immediately follow the right-of-the-firstborn passage also support that Ezra should have inherited the chief priesthood. The verses (Deut 21:18–19) read, "If someone has a stubborn and rebellious son who will not obey his father and mother, who does not heed them when they discipline him, then his father and his mother shall take hold of him and bring him out to the elders . . ." There the parents accuse the boy of being a stubborn, disobedient, overindulgent drunkard. The sentence to be meted out in such cases, says Deuteronomy, should be death by stoning. Although there are no anagrams, the coding marks Seraiah as the father and designates the wayward son as Jozadak.³ Thus, according to Deut 21, the next chief priest should be the elder brother Ezra. If followed, this opinion would have decided the matter for the older Ezra over the younger Jozadak, but events brought complications. Jerusalem's fall, the chief priest's execution, young Jozadak's deportation,

---

1. Kavanagh, *Exilic Code*, 74. The Jacob material is in Gen 25, 27–32, 34, 35, 46, 47, and 49. Only chapter 49 appears to have been written by Jacob the prophet.

2. Twenty single-interval spellings of Seraiah (using למאו, שריה, and ניתחא) occur in the passage, along with nine Ezra coded spellings that employ הנאר and רככה.

3. Ten consecutive למאו "Seraiah" spellings start at word 18-6 of Deut 21 and eight more begin at word 20-8. These are A and B values. "Jehozadak," an alternate to Jozadak, has A and AAA rated athbash spellings: סרקזש with four consecutive spellings and רסענו with seven, beginning at words 20-6 and 20-3, respectively.

and the temple's destruction seem to have overwhelmed any traditional succession plan for the highest priestly office.

Scholars generally agree that chapters 5–28 constitute the original book of Deuteronomy.[4] Five verses within Deut 21 (a) were written during the early Exile, (b) addressed priestly succession, and (c) were strongly on Ezra's side. Can these clues from Deut 21:15–19 help to uncover the origins of the book of Deuteronomy?

Jozadak Anagrams Tell Exile's Story

To this writer's knowledge, no commentator has recognized that an abortive Cyrus-led revolt took place in Judah at the end of the 570s. (A partial exception to this is set forth in Sidney Smith's remarkable 1944 book on Second Isaiah. Smith said that major portions of Isa 40–55 described Cyrus's successful campaign in the later 540s that freed Syria, Palestine, and Arabia from Babylonian rule.[5] Smith was on the right track. If there were two uprisings—one in 570 and the other in the 540s—Smith was right about the later one. But if the Cyrus-led revolt of 570 is the only one, then Smith's reading of Second Isaiah is incorrect in two particulars. First, the uprising was several decades earlier, and second, it was a bloody failure.) That discussion aside, until scholars take account of the 570 catastrophe, considerable portions of HS must remain without context or assigned authorship.

Fortunately, Jozadak biblical anagrams can present us with a participant's-eye view of the period between Jerusalem's fall in 586 and the revolt's aftermath some twenty years later. Scripture contains 279 Jozadak BAs, concealed in most books of the Hebrew Bible. Our first task was to group passages containing those BAs into such categories as army, rebuilding, disputes, and the like. Often we reached into adjacent verses to include texts with related BAs such as Cyrus, Ezra, Jacob, Asaiah, and Baruch. An organizing principle has been whether, in our opinion, the passage originated before, during, or after the revolt. Few Jozadak anagrams have remained without assignment, and the categories seemed almost to suggest themselves.[6]

---

4. Weinfeld, "Deuteronomy," 171.

5. Smith, *Isaiah*, 49–75.

6. "Zedekiah," the name of the last king of Judah, has the most Jozadak BAs. However, because the king and Jozadak were contemporaries, it is difficult to determine which the

The Shaphan Group

Some Jozadak-BA passages follow. First Chronicles 6:14 [Heb. 5:40–41] says, "Jehozadak [Jozadak BA] went into exile when the LORD sent Judah and Jerusalem into exile by the hand of Nebuchadnezzar." Later, in separate pronouncements, Jeremiah used anagrams to place Jehozadak in northern Egypt: "The word that came to Jeremiah for all the Judeans living in the land of Egypt, at Migdol, at Tahpanhes [Jozadak, Jacob BAs], at Memphis, and in the land of Pathros" (Jer 44:1; see also 46:14). Jozadak, then, had made it from his exile in Mesopotamia to northern Egypt, where he joined Jacob and other refugees from Judah who had fled the oncoming Nebuchadnezzar.

According to Josephus, the Babylonian king moved against Egypt five years after he destroyed Jerusalem, or about 581 BCE.[7] Although battles were fought and a pharaoh died, ultimately the Babylonians were forced to withdraw. It is reasonably certain that Judahites fought for the Egyptians, for Jeremiah urged them to do so. The prophet warned about "the coming of King Nebuchadrezzar [Baruch, Jacob, Qohelet BAs] of Babylon to attack the land of Egypt: Declare [Asaiah, Qohelet BAs] in Egypt, and proclaim [Asaiah, Qohelet BAs] in Migdol; proclaim in Memphis and Tahpanhes [Jozadak, Jacob BAs]; Say, 'Take your stations [Jacob BA] and be ready, for the sword shall devour those around you'" (Jer 46:13–14). The fighting would have created a seasoned cadre of Jewish troops in the Jewish settlements in Northern Egypt. Their leaders would have been the people whom Jeremiah addressed: Jacob, Jozadak, Baruch, Asaiah, and Qohelet. Under Josiah, Asaiah held the title of servant of the king (2 Kgs 22:12), and this book's final chapter will show that he was a leading figure in the Exile. As to Qohelet, he may or may not be the person to whom Ecclesiastes is attributed.

Was it common to travel from exile communities in Mesopotamia to Palestine or Egypt? Certainly it was done, perhaps even routinely. The neo-Babylonians marched armies across the Fertile Crescent, and Jozadak's journey is exhibit A for individuals. The Chronicles passage quoted above says that Jozadak went into exile "when the LORD sent Judah and Jerusalem into exile by the hand of Nebuchadnezzar." And we know that five years later Jozadak was at Tahpanhes in northern Egypt, because Jeremiah used BAs to place him there. We soon shall learn that

---

author intended to signify. For this reason, we shall withhold discussion of Jozadak BAs in the name "Zedekiah."

7. *Ant* 9:7.

Ezra and Jozadak BAs Sketch Exile's History

people, information, and funds journeyed with facility between east and west.

Jozadak a Leader

Table 2.1 in the previous chapter gave the surprisingly high totals of single text words that housed multiple BAs of Jozadak, Ezra, Jacob, Baruch, and Cyrus. The shared text words were statistically significant for each pair: Jozadak-Ezra, Jozadak-Jacob, Ezra-Jacob, etc. That is, word associations pairing any two of the five were intentionally made. In establishing that Jozadak was a leader of Judah's exiles, we shall concentrate upon such words as "enroll," "register," and "oversee." These are derived from the stem פקד, which was beloved by those who wrote the book of Numbers. One form of the word פקדיהם ("enrolled") contains BAs of Jacob, Ezra, and Jozadak. It appears twenty times, all within Numbers. The book's opening chapter has a dozen such spellings. Others are in Num 3, 4, and 26. Clearly Jacob and the two brothers are up to something.

The first modification prefixes a *waw* to form ופקדיהם, "as enrolled." This adds a second Ezra BA (וקים) to the text word along with the Jacob and Jehozadak BAs already there. That spelling appears nine times in Num 2, once in Num 3, and three times in Num 26.

The next step in this progression is to substitute the *waw* with the prefix *lamed*, forming לפקדיהם ("to register"). This accommodates a brand new Cyrus spelling (פלדך) but drops one of the Ezra BAs. That is, each of those spellings contained BAs for Jozadak, Jacob, Ezra, and Cyrus. The new form announces nine times that Cyrus had joined the group (in Exod 30:12 and Num 3:43 as well as Num 26:18, 22, 25, 27, 37, 43, and 47).

Two other forms will complete our survey of פקד. In Neh 3:31, המפקד with a changed sequence spells an athbash of "Jozadak." Those five letters concealed no Jacob, Ezra, or Cyrus BAs. Tellingly, the Jozadak anagram is translated "muster," and is paired with "gate" to form "Muster Gate." The context of Neh 3 is reconstruction, and the author is saying to informed readers that Jozadak had worked at that very spot a century before. (We shall talk later about Jozadak and temple construction.) Scripture's other use of this stem is המפקדים, translated as "oversight" or "overseers" in the Second Kings and Chronicles verses describing Josiah's temple repairs (2 Kgs 22:5, 9; 2 Chr 34:10, 17). Since the Hebrew word

51

in Chronicles and Kings houses BAs of Jacob and of the two brothers, they may have composed or edited the Second Kings original. At any rate, Kings and Chronicles use פקד in the same way that Numbers does.

The Cyrus BA additions in Exodus and Numbers are all-important. Cyrus's early involvement with the Jews is the fulcrum upon which exilic history swings. Before him, life in Palestine and Babylon was unpleasant but at least tolerable; after him, the Jews became a persecuted people. We estimate the date when Cyrus the Great initially appeared in Scripture by coming from two directions. The first direction depends upon the date of Nebuchadnezzar's foray against Egypt. Josephus says that the Babylonian invasion started five years after the fall of Jerusalem, or about 581.[8] Jewish refugees in Egypt would certainly have fought against Nebuchadnezzar. The campaign must have concluded in a year or so, leaving the Jewish settlements in northern Egypt with a cadre of experienced fighters. Using the Egyptian sanctuary, in the early 570s Baruch, Jacob, Ezra, Jozadak, and other leaders began assembling funds and people to retake Jerusalem. Around the same time, they apparently reached out to Cyrus, who would have been in his early twenties.[9]

Now here is an approach to the Cyrus question from another, later, direction. This author has estimated that the best date for the Suffering Servant's execution was a few months after the solar eclipse of January 5, 569 BCE.[10] The prophet Ezekiel died as a substitute king, and his death ended a persecution that followed a Cyrus-led uprising in Judah in the later 570s. This might push back his recruitment to, say, 578–576. (Cyrus and the Suffering Servant are discussed in two previous books.[11] At this writing, there is no indication that OT scholars know of these matters.)

So far we have concentrated upon anagrams derived from the פקד stem. Now we turn to the opening chapters of Numbers, adding coding and a range of other BAs for Cyrus, Baruch, Jacob, Ezra, and Jozadak. Numbers 1–4 contain statistically significant coding or BAs for Baruch, Jacob, Ezra, and Jozadak, while chapters 2 and 3 have significant Cyrus coding. These Numbers chapters deal with men fit for war, with arranging

---

8. *Ant* 9:7.

9. Mallowan in "Cyrus," 9, picks 598 as the birth year. Although young, Cyrus probably was experienced in war. For comparison, at eighteen Alexander commanded a wing of his father's army.

10. Kavanagh, *Exilic Code*, 111.

11. Ibid., 33–36; and Kavanagh, *Secrets*, 359–73.

encampments, and with Levitical clans.¹² We suggest that future learned discussions of the book of Numbers take into account the influence of Cyrus, Jacob, Baruch, and the two brothers.

Jozadak and Funds

The ancients soon learned that war costs money. Anagrams leave no doubt that Jozadak was deeply involved in fundraising to recruit troops, repair the Jerusalem temple, and construct defenses. These words sound like a tax upon households: "a beka a head (that is, half a shekel, measured by the sanctuary shekel), for everyone who was counted [Jozadak, Ezra, Jacob BAs] in the census, from twenty years old and upward, for six hundred three thousand . . . men" (Exod 38:26). Not unexpectedly, contributions carried divine sanction: "Throughout your generations [Jozadak BA] you shall give to the LORD a donation from the first of your batch of dough" (Num 15:21). The following quotations imply that the cash came from temple treasury sources, perhaps hidden from the Babylonians prior to Jerusalem's siege. "'Your servants have emptied out the money that was found in the house, and have delivered it into the hand of the workers who have oversight [Jozadak, Jacob, Ezra BAs] of the house of the LORD;'" and "They delivered it to the workers who had the oversight [Jozadak, Jacob, Ezra BAs] of the house of the LORD" (2 Kgs 22:9, 2 Chr 34:10). Second Chronicles 34:17 is similar.

Job (twice) and a psalmist conveyed their support: "if the Almighty is your gold [Jozadak BA] and your precious silver"; "they may pile it up, but the just [Jozadak BA] will wear [Daniel BA] it, and the innocent will divide the silver"; and "the righteous [Jozadak BA] are generous and keep giving" (Job 22:25, 27:17; Ps 37:21). The Daniel BA hints that Jews in Babylon were involved. Not unexpectedly, money led to argument: "The wicked borrow, and do not pay back, but the righteous [Jozadak BA] are generous and keep giving" (Ps 37:21).

---

12. Other Numbers chapters with significant Cyrus coding are 7, 19, 26, and 34. Surprisingly, no chapter in that book contains significant Cyrus BAs. Other Numbers chapters with significant Baruch BAs are 7, 10, 26, 28, 29, and 36. Jacob additions are 7, 10, 19, 23, 26, 28, 29, and 34. Ezra also has 8, 17, 20, 26, 28–30, and 36. Finally, other significant Jozadak chapters in Numbers are 15, 19, 26, 29, 34, and 36. Of course, Baruch, Jacob, Ezra, and Jozadak have significant coding or BAs in chapters 1–4.

The Shaphan Group

The amount of money that Cyrus the Persian must have received is surprising. Perhaps the Jews were also hiring a cohort of his troops. The story in Gen 43 of Joseph, the sacks, and his brothers concerns money for Cyrus: "because of the money, replaced in our sacks [Jozadak, Cyrus BAs] . . . so that he may have an opportunity to fall upon us, to make slaves [Daniel BA] of us and take our donkeys." Does the Daniel BA confirm that the money came from Babylonian Jews? From the same Gen 43 account, "we opened [Jacob BA] our sacks [Jozadak, Cyrus BAs], and there was each one's money in the top of his sack [Cyrus BA], our money in full weight. . . . We do not know who put our money in our sacks [Jozadak, Cyrus BAs]" (Gen 43:18, 21–23). In the next chapter we find, "the money that we found at the top [Jozadak, Cyrus BAs] of our sacks, we brought back to you from the land of Canaan" (Gen 44:8). Canaan, then, was apparently the source of these funds.

Later, with Cyrus still on the scene, the money seems to have been earmarked for reconstruction of the temple: "workers who have the oversight [Jozadak, Jacob, Ezra BAs] of the house of the LORD; let them give it [the money] to . . . the carpenters [Cyrus BA], . . . to the masons [Cyrus BA]" (2 Kgs 22:5–6). A census was decreed to apportion giving: "take a census of the Israelites to register [Jozadak, Cyrus, Ezra, Jacob BAs] them . . . all of them shall give a ransom for their lives to the LORD, so that no plague may come upon them for being registered [Jozadak, Ezra, Jacob BAs] . . . half a shekel according to the shekel of the sanctuary" (Exod 30:11–13).

Both Jeremiah and Ezekiel condemned the entire operation. Jeremiah prophesied, "Because you trusted in your strongholds and your treasures [Jozadak, Cyrus, Baruch, Saris BAs], you also shall be taken; Chemosh shall go out into exile, with his priests [Jacob BA] . . ." (Jer 48:7). And from Mesopotamia, Ezekiel wrote, "by your . . . understanding [Daniel BA] you have amassed wealth for yourself, and have gathered gold and silver into your treasuries [Jozadak, Saris, Baruch, Cyrus BAs]" (Ezek 28:4). "Saris," which means eunuch, probably was a Daniel pseudonym.

Sixth-Century Covenant

Once Cyrus had joined the Israelites, a covenant was drawn. The parties included at least Jozadak, Ezra, Jacob, King Jehoiachin, Daniel, and Asaiah (the former official of Josiah). Scripture's master passage is the covenant between God and Abraham in Gen 17. "'I will establish [Ezra, Jacob BAs] my covenant between me and you, and your offspring after you throughout their generations [Jozadak BA], for an everlasting covenant, to be God to you... And I will give to you... the land where you are [Cyrus BA] now an alien, all the land of Canaan, for a perpetual holding; and I will be their God... This is my covenant, which you shall keep, between [Jehoiachin BA] me and you and your offspring after you: Every male among you shall be circumcised'" (Gen 17:7–10). Cyrus got Canaan "for a perpetual holding" while accepting the sway there of Elohim. Jehoiachin, presumably *in absentia*, agreed to circumcise his offspring. The two brothers and Jacob actively participated in the covenant.

Elsewhere, an Exodus passage settled that Ezra and his sons were to kindle lamps outside the inner sanctuary. Jozadak used an anagram to sign off on this matter: "In the tent of meeting, outside the curtain that is before the covenant, Aaron [Ezra BA] and his sons shall tend it from evening to morning before the LORD. It shall be a perpetual ordinance to be observed throughout their generations [Jozadak BA] by the Israelites" (Exod 27:21; Lev 24:3 is similar). In Exod 31, Jehoiachin and Jozadak agreed to keep the sabbath "as a perpetual covenant" (Exod 31:13, 16), and in Lev 23:31, Daniel concurred: "You shall do no work: it is a statute forever throughout your generations [Jozadak] in all your settlements [Daniel]."

Finally, Asaiah joined Jozadak in establishing the festival of booths to commemorate when the Lord "brought them out of the land of Egypt." "You shall keep it as a festival to the LORD seven days in the year; you shall keep it in the seventh [Asaiah BA] month as a statute forever throughout your generations [Jozadak BA]" (Lev 23:41).

This chapter is but a partial Cook's tour of the Exile from the fall of Jerusalem in 586 to the mid-570s. In it we seek to feature some of the events in which Jozadak was involved, including Jozadak's role in assembling an army, probably in Northern Egypt.

Jozadak Anagrams and Israel's Army

Exodus 12:17 reads, "You shall observe the festival of unleavened bread, for on this very day I brought your companies [Cyrus BA] out of the land of Egypt: you shall observe this day throughout your generations [Jozadak BA] as a perpetual ordinance." The "festival" of unleavened bread may

The Shaphan Group

have been instituted to celebrate the sixth-century departure of an Israeli army from Egypt, or it may overlay a far earlier tradition.[13] "Your generations," לדרתיכם, conceals דתללם, an athbash of Jozadak. Genesis 17, as well as Exodus, Leviticus, and Numbers use "generations" thirty-eight times, each of them to form a Jozadak BA. The word "companies" in Exod 12:17 (which can also be translated "battle array") houses a Cyrus anagram. In turn, this tells us that Cyrus joined the Israelites, perhaps near Sinai, soon after they left Egypt.

How could Cyrus the Persian participate in the festival of unleavened bread? Immediately following another Jozadak anagram, Scripture says, "The LORD said to Moses and Aaron [Ezra, Jacob BAs]: This is the ordinance for the passover: no foreigner shall eat of it, but any slave [or servant] who has been purchased may eat of it after he has been circumcised [Cyrus BA]" (Exod 12:43–44). Cyrus was a foreigner and his services had indeed been purchased. While it is far from clear that he underwent circumcision, he could have. The mixture of passover, Cyrus, and battle are addressed in the following verse: "Anyone of you or your descendants [Jozadak BA] who is unclean through touching a corpse [Cyrus BA], or is away on a journey, shall still keep the passover to the LORD" (Num 9:10).

A longer quote from the book of Numbers is given below. It begins a tally by tribes of "everyone able to go to war" and is thick with BAs. This passage has four of the dozen words with a פקד stem words that host Jozadak, Ezra, and Jacob anagrams. Multiple Baruch and Qohelet BAs are also present. The text's tribal totals are inflated by at least a factor of ten, so those words carry a message that remains hidden from us. Alternatively, these passages could be a rework of an ancient census.

> ...those enrolled [Jozadak, Ezra, Jacob BAs] of the tribe of Reuben [Jacob BA] were forty-six thousand five hundred. The descendants of Simeon [Qohelet BA], their lineage, in their clans [Baruch BA] ... every male from twenty years old and upward, everyone able to go to war: those enrolled [Jozadak, Ezra, Jacob BAs] of the tribe of Simeon [Qohelet BA] were fifty-nine thousand three hundred. The descendants of Gad, their lineage, in their clans [Baruch BA] ... from twenty years old and upward, everyone able to go to war: those enrolled [Jozadak, Ezra, Jacob BAs] of the tribe of Gad were forty-five thousand six hundred fifty. The descendants of Judah,

---

13. JSB notes on 127 that the Hebrew text omits "festival" and literally reads "You shall observe the unleavened bread."

their lineage, in their clans [Baruch BA] ... from twenty years old and upward, everyone able to go to war: those enrolled [Jozadak, Ezra, Jacob BAs] of the tribe of Judah were seventy-[Qohelet BA] four thousand six hundred. (Num 1:21–27)

Much of the rest of Num 1 is similar. It is repetitive, formulaic, and heavy with anagrams. This is a Priestly Source chapter, and we have identified Ezra as the P Source. The passage above contains four of his BA signatures, but it also holds equal totals of Jacob and Jozadak anagrams. Jacob—Second Isaiah—would not have written something so labored as Num 1, but possibly Ezra and his brother Jozadak collaborated on this and other Numbers P-Source chapters. Authorship aside, this text is exilic. It also is about an Israelite army gathered in Egypt or its surrounding areas.

Numbers 2 deals with individual military leaders. If anything, the chapter exceeds Num 1 in total anagrams. Variations of פקד, usually accompanied by the word for army, crowd the chapter. They carry three to four anagrams each and always include Jozadak.[14] For example, "... with a company as enrolled [Jozadak, Jacob, two Ezra BAs] of fifty-nine thousand three hundred. Then the tribe of Gad ... with a company as enrolled [Jozadak, Jacob, two Ezra BAs] of forty-five thousand six hundred fifty. The total enrollment [Jozadak, Jacob, Ezra BAs] of the camp of Reuben [Jacob BA], by companies ..." (Num 2:13–16).

Numbers 3 may contain an accurate estimate of the army's size. "The total enrollment ... counting [Ezra, Jacob, Cyrus BAs] the number of names, was twenty-two thousand two hundred seventy-three" (Num 3:43). That same chapter also features thirty—repeat thirty—Baruch BAs derived from the word for clan or family, and Num 26 easily tops that with almost *one hundred*. Baruch must have taken command alongside of Cyrus. In chapter 26, Cyrus BAs usually share the same פקד form with BAs of Jozadak, Ezra, and Jacob, though sometimes only the three Israelite names are encoded.[15]

---

14. Num 2:9, 13, 15, 16, 19, 21, 23, 24, 26, 28, 30, 31.

15. BAs of the three Israelites and Cyrus: Num 26:18, 22, 25, 27, 34, 43, 47; BAs of the three Israelites without Cyrus: Num 26:7, 34, 50, 62.

The Shaphan Group

Wilderness Disputes

Continuing our tracking of Jozadak BAs, once the army cleared Egypt, disputes inevitably arose. In this argument, Asaiah and Jozadak were on opposite sides: "Suppose two persons have a dispute and enter into litigation, and the judges decide between them, declaring one to be in the right [Jozadak BA] and the other to be in the wrong [Asaiah BA]"; and also, ". . . condemning the guilty [Asaiah BA] by bringing their conduct on their own head, and vindicating the righteous [Jozadak BA] by rewarding them according to their righteousness [Cyrus BA]" (Deut 25:1, 1 Kgs 8:32). Second Chronicles 6:23 has virtually the same wording as 1 Kgs 8 except that it substitutes a Daniel BA for that of Asaiah. One source of dispute could have been kingship, as the following suggests: "'We have added to all our sins [Jozadak, Jacob BAs] the evil of demanding a king for ourselves.'" Baruch might have been the candidate, as this author has proposed before.[16] Did Jozadak support Baruch? Proverbs offers this post-mortem: "When the tempest passes [Baruch BA], the wicked are no more, but the righteous [Jozadak BA] are established forever" (Prov 10:25). And again, "When the wicked are in authority, transgression increases, but the righteous [Jozadak, Jacob, Ezra BAs] will look upon their downfall" (Prov 29:16). Jacob and the two brothers may have allied themselves against Baruch.

The Proverbs author had used the same "righteous" spelling before: "The wicked flee when no one pursues, but the righteous [Jozadak, Ezra, Jacob BAs] are as bold as a lion" (Prov 28:1). Another famous phrase that also involved Jozadak was, "Look at the proud! Their spirit is not right in them, but the righteous [Jozadak BA] live by their faith" (Hab 2:4).[17] (This Habakkuk phrase was a favorite of the Reformation reformers.) In the same vein, "The ways of the LORD are right [Jozadak, Jacob, Ezra BAs], and the upright walk in them, but transgressors [Jehoiachin, Qohelet BAs] stumble in them" (Hos 14:9, H10). As to alignment in these undefined disputes, Jozadak, Jacob, and Ezra always stood together with Cyrus, while Asaiah, Jehoiachin, Daniel, Qohelet, and sometimes Baruch were opposed.

Critics of the Jozadak-Ezra-Jacob consortium certainly included the two great prophets Jeremiah and Ezekiel. To them, the military adven-

---

16. Kavanagh, *Secrets*, 365.
17. Other pro-Jozadak verses are in Pss 86:17; 119:53; Prov 21:26; 29:6; Isa 45:25.

ture was deathly folly: "Because you trusted in your strongholds and your treasures [Jozadak, Cyrus, Baruch, Saris BAs], you also shall be taken; Chemosh shall go out into exile, with his priests [Jacob] and his attendants"; "'The LORD make you like Zedekiah [Jozadak, Cyrus BAs] and Ahab, whom the king of Babylon roasted in the fire'"; and "By . . . your understanding [Daniel BA] you have amassed wealth for yourself, and have gathered gold and silver into your treasuries [Jozadak, Saris, Baruch, Cyrus BAs]" (Jer 48:7, 29:22; Ezek 28:4). And the person or persons masquerading as Hosea, Amos, and Micah published the following passages, "You have plowed [Cyrus BA] wickedness . . . Because you have trusted in your power and in the multitude of your warriors [Baruch, Cyrus, Jehoiachin BAs], therefore the tumult of war shall rise against your people, and all your fortresses [Jozadak BA] shall be destroyed"; "The time is surely coming upon you, when they shall take you away with hooks, even the last [Jozadak, Jacob, Jehoiachin BAs] of you with fishhooks [Baruch BA]"; and "I will cut off the cities of your land and throw down all your strongholds [Jozadak BA]" (Hos 10:13, Amos 4:2, Mic 5:11 [Heb 10]). We can date every one of these dire pronouncements to the later 570s. Clearly, Jozadak, Baruch, Jacob, and of course Cyrus were deeply involved in the uprising and would pay terrible penalties. Jehoiachin, too, played his role, though it probably was from Babylon.

Jozadak's War Anagrams

Unlike their Assyrian predecessors, the Babylonians chose not to garrison their western conquests. We can assume, therefore, that in late 571 or early 570, after Nebuchadnezzar had concluded the siege of Tyre and closed out his second Egyptian campaign, he withdrew his forces from the west.[18] This, in turn, opened a window of opportunity for Cyrus and the Israelite army to move into Canaan.

Israel's neighbors were the first to test the newly formed army. An Amorite king summoned his allies: "'Come up and help me [Jozadak BA], and let us attack Gibeon [Daniel BA]; for it has made peace with Joshua [Asaiah BA] and with the Israelites'"; "The Gibeonites [Daniel BA] sent to Joshua [Asaiah BA] . . . saying, 'Do not abandon your servants

---

18. See Katzenstein, "Tyre," 690, on dating the siege. Ezek 29:17–20, which bears a date of April 571, indicates that the siege of Tyre was over and that Nebuchadnezzar had turned his attention to Egypt.

The Shaphan Group

[Daniel BA]; come up to us quickly, and save [Asaiah BA] us, and help us [Jozadak BA]; for all the kings of the Amorites . . . are gathered against us'" (Josh 10:4, 6). Also, "Moab said to the elders of Midian, 'This horde will now lick up all that is around [Jozadak, Baruch BAs] us . . .'" (Num 22:4). Cyrus seemed unrestrained by ancient treaties: "Gibeonites [two Daniel BAs] were . . . of the remnant of the Amorites; although the people of Israel had sworn to spare them, Saul had tried to wipe [Cyrus BA] them out" (2 Sam 21:2). Cyrus also helped the Israelites settle old scores: the Samuel of Scripture said, "'The LORD has helped [Jozadak BA] us.' So the Philistines [Cyrus BA] were subdued [Jehoiachin BA] and did not again enter the territory of Israel; the hand of the LORD was against the Philistines [Daniel BA] all the days of Samuel" (1 Sam 7:12–13). Gibeon, the Amorites, Moab, Midian, and Philistia make an impressive list. The main event against the formidable Nebuchadnezzar, however, had yet to be fought.

It appears that the Israelites gained possession of Jerusalem, though no Jozadak anagrams say this directly. The best source seems to be the Melchizedek passage in Gen 14. Verses 16–23 tell how the king of Salem (presumably Cyrus and Jerusalem) receives homage and tithes from Abram. He, in turn, splits up booty with the king of Sodom (probably Edom's king). Those verses contain anagrams for Cyrus (five), Baruch (two), and Ezra and Asaiah (one each). Aside from Ezra, these were Israel's war leaders. Reconstruction of the temple apparently began soon after Jerusalem fell: "They would give the money that was weighed out into the hands of the workers who had the oversight [Jozadak, Ezra, Jacob BAs] of the house of the LORD; then they paid it out to the carpenters and the builders who worked on the house of the LORD" (2 Kgs 12:11 [Heb 12]). Other passages are similar.[19]

Very likely, worship was soon reinstituted on the site of Solomon's destroyed temple—as signaled by the following: "The LORD has brought forth our vindication [Jozadak, Baruch, Jehoiachin BAs]; come, let us declare in Zion the work of the LORD our God" (Jer 51:10). But passages from the Minor Prophets objected to overblown religious ceremonies and declared that destruction lay ahead: "'Is not the day of the LORD darkness, not light, and gloom [Asaiah BA] with no brightness in it? I hate, I despise [Cyrus BA] your festivals, and I take no delight in your solemn assemblies

---

19. 2 Chr 34:10, 17 are rebuilding verses that contain Jozadak, Ezra, and Jacob BAs. See also Neh 3:31, 6:16.

[Jozadak BA]'"; and "'Shall I come before [Cyrus, Baruch BAs] him with burnt offerings, with calves [Jozadak BA] a year old? Will the LORD be pleased with thousands of rams, with ten thousands of rivers of oil? Shall I give my firstborn [Baruch BA] for my transgression, the fruit of my body for the sin of my soul?'" (Amos 5:20, Mic 6:7). The combination of Jozadak, Baruch, and Cyrus BAs fix these texts as written in 570 BCE, give or take a year.

Jozadak and Ezra Agree on Priesthood

Even before Israelite forces took Jerusalem, Ezra and Jozadak seem to have agreed upon Ezra's preeminence in the priesthood. The following might date from the middle to later 570s. "You shall anoint Aaron [Ezra BA] and his sons, and consecrate them, in order that they may serve me as priests. You shall say to the Israelites, 'This shall be my holy anointing oil throughout your generations [Jozadak BA]'" (Exod 30:30–31). In the text above, the Lord addressed Moses about Aaron (with its Ezra BA) and the instruction closed with "throughout your generations," with its Jozadak BA.[20] Readers across the Diaspora would understand that Jozadak had concurred with the sacerdotal power ceded to his older brother.

This next set of Exodus anagrams makes Ezra's high priesthood hereditary. The text says, "You shall bring Aaron [Ezra BA] and his sons to the entrance of the tent of meeting . . . and put on Aaron [Ezra BA] the sacred vestments, and you shall anoint him and consecrate him, so that he may serve me as priest. You shall bring his sons also and put tunics on them, and anoint them, as you anointed their father, that they may serve me as priests: and *their anointing shall admit them to a perpetual priesthood throughout all generations* [Jozadak BA] to come" (Exod 40:12–15, emphasis added). These verses go a long way toward explaining how control of the priesthood passed from Zadokite-Levite hands to Aaronite domination after the Exile, a thing of no small importance.

Another matter concerns the tabernacle, the tent sanctuary that the Israelites used as a place of worship from the Exodus until Solomon built his temple, which may in turn have housed the tabernacle. It appears that Jacob, Ezra, and Jozadak constructed a tabernacle not long after leaving

---

20. Other texts that follow the pattern of Ezra BA-priestly privilege-Jozadak BA concurrence are Exod 27:21; Lev 7:35–36, 21:17, 24:3; Num 10:8. Exod 31:13 and 16 are similar, though the Ezra BA is not immediately nearby.

The Shaphan Group

Egypt. A Jozadak BA preceded these words: "In the first month in the second year, on the first [Jacob, Ezra BAs] day of the month, the tabernacle was set up. Moses set up [Ezra BA] the tabernacle; he laid its bases, and set up its frames, and put in its poles, and raised up its pillars" (Exod 40:17–18).[21] Perhaps this was a second tabernacle used during a second exodus from Egypt and then installed a second time atop Jerusalem's temple mount. But another alternative is that this was the only tabernacle fashioned during a wilderness trek by the Israelites and then installed at the Jerusalem site—all during the sixth-century Exile rather than during a far earlier Exodus.

Babylonians Capture Jerusalem, Jozadak

Nebuchadnezzar in Babylon would have kept himself well informed about developments in the west. Probably he heard about the Israelites gathering funds and men, and certainly his informants would have reported the movements of young Cyrus and his troops. Very likely, as soon as fighting commenced in Canaan, say in 570 BCE, authorities began to imprison Jews in Babylonia. We have estimated that Ezekiel's execution occurred early in 569, though it could have been a year or so after that. Cyrus, Baruch, and the rest must have been feverishly fortifying Jerusalem and other settlements against Nebuchadnezzar's arrival, for the correspondence via Scripture mentions strongholds. Jeremiah warned, "The destroyer of Moab has come up against you; he has destroyed your strongholds [Jozadak BA]" (Jer 48:18).[22]

We have mentioned the difficulty of looking in "Zedekiah" for BAs of Jozadak. However, because of the wealth of anagrams that this particular Jeremiah passage contains, we offer it here: ". . . evil in the sight of the LORD, just as Jehoiakim [Ezra, Jacob BAs] had done. Indeed [Saris BA], Jerusalem [Daniel BA] and Judah so angered the LORD that he expelled them from his presence. Zedekiah [Jozadak BA] rebelled against the king of Babylon. And in the ninth [Asaiah BA] year of his reign, in the tenth [Asaiah BA] month, on the tenth [Jehoiachin BA] day of the month, King Nebuchadrezzar [Baruch, Jacob, Qohelet BAs] of Babylon came with all his army against Jerusalem, and they laid siege to it . . ." (Jer 52:2–4).

21. "First month of the second year" could connect the tabernacle to the date when the Israelites left Egypt, which might have been 572 or 571.

22. Nebuchadnezzar had pacified Moab about 581. Josephus *Ant* 9:7.

Ezra and Jozadak BAs Sketch Exile's History

While this Jeremiah text describes Jerusalem's siege in 586, we think that the author meant it to apply to the uprising sixteen years later. The Jeremiah version is tighter than its parallel in Second Kings, and alters the spelling of Nebuchadnezzar so as to add anagrams for both Baruch and Jacob. Although the siege probably was short, it was long enough for Jozadak or someone close to him to write, "Our eyes failed, ever watching vainly for help [Jozadak]; we were watching eagerly for a nation [surely Egypt] that could not save" (Lam 4:17).

Jozadak's Travail

The Babylonians must have captured Jozadak when they stormed the Jerusalem site. Dispersed Jews, whose hopes must surely have soared, would have been in despair. Ezekiel expressed it: "Say to the house of Israel, Thus you have said: 'Our transgressions and our sins [Jozadak, Jacob BAs] weigh upon us, and we waste away because of them; how then can we live?'" (Ezek 33:10). From Third Isaiah came these quotations: "Our transgressions before you are many, and our sins [Jozadak, Jacob, Ezra BAs] testify against us"; and "We have all become like one who is unclean, and all our righteous [Jozadak, Baruch, Jehoiachin BAs] deeds are like a filthy cloth. We all fade like a leaf, and our iniquities, like the wind, take us away" (Isa 59:12, 64:6). Daniel 9:16–17 said, "Because of our sins and the iniquities of our ancestors, Jerusalem and your people have become a disgrace [Qohelet BA] among all our neighbors [Jozadak, Baruch BA]. LORD, let your face shine upon your desolated sanctuary."

Several anagrams in Psalms allude to prison: "They rise in the darkness as a light for the upright; they are gracious, merciful, and righteous [Jozadak BA]"; and "Even there your hand shall lead me, and your right hand shall hold me fast [Jozadak BA]" (Pss 112:4, 139:10). His captors are certain to have applied torture. The word אנחתי, which means "my groaning," is an athbash anagram for Jozadak. In Psalms, Job, Jeremiah, and Lamentations, the authors worked that word into their texts to highlight the travail of their subjects. More than once, in this writer's view, that author was Jozadak himself. Jeremiah said, "'Woe is me! The LORD has added sorrow to my pain; I am weary with my groaning [Jozadak BA], and I find no rest.'" Lamentations reads, ". . . because of all my transgressions; for my groans [Jozadak BA] are many and my heart is faint." Job has two such anagrams: "His hand is heavy despite my groaning [Jozadak

The Shaphan Group

BA]," and "Why is light given to one who cannot [Cyrus BA] see the way, whom God has fenced in? For my sighing [Jozadak BA] comes like my bread, and my groanings are poured out like water" (Jer 45:3; Lam 1:22; Job 23:2; 3:23). The last Job quotation above features bread and water, as well as the Cyrus anagram. Jozadak's tormentors would have wanted to know all about the Persian.

Next, in this extraordinary text, Jozadak confesses to the outside world that he has told the Babylonians everything: "O LORD, all my longing is known to you; my sighing [Jozadak BA] is not hidden [Cyrus BA] from you" (Ps 38:9 [Heb 10]). In Ps 6:6 [Heb 7], Jozadak reveals that Daniel is also in prison: "I am weary with my moaning [Jozadak BA]; every night I flood my bed with tears [Daniel BA]; I drench my couch with my weeping."[23] Daniel might have been captured in Babylon rather than at Jerusalem. If it was in Babylon, he would at the least have been implicated in raising funds for the revolt.

Jozadak's Death

How did Jozadak die? Anagrams hint that the Babylonians might have executed him as a substitute king. The opening chapter of the Holiness Code says, ". . . so that they may no longer offer their sacrifices [Jehoiachin BA] for goat-demons, to whom they prostitute themselves. This shall [Saris BA] be a statute forever to them throughout their generations [Jozadak BA]" (Lev 17:7). The word שעיר, "goat-demon," can mean a he-goat for a sin offering as well as a pagan idol.[24] A substitute king was indeed a sin offering and the substitute had to swear oaths before the pagan idol of the sun god.[25] The association of that word with Jehoiachin and Jozadak could have implied that Jozadak met or would meet the same end as Jehoiachin, who was executed as a substitute king.[26] Babylonian kings were enthroned anew during the annual New Year's Festival, and at one point in the swearing ceremony the chief priest would slap the kneeling king-to-be in the face. We do not know whether this was also part of Babylon's substitute-king ritual. However, in view of this phrase, slapping

---

23. Psalm 102:5 [Heb 6] may also have been written by Jozadak himself: "Because of my loud groaning [אנחתי, Jozadak BA] my bones cling to my skin."
24. BDB, 972.
25. Parpola II, xxiv.
26. Kavanagh, *Exilic Code*, 43.

probably was an integral part of the substitute ceremony: "Then Zedekiah [Jozadak BA] son of Chenaanah came up to Micaiah, slapped him on the cheek, and said..." (1 Kgs 22:24). Second Chronicles 18:23 uses the same words.

One can make a strong case that the Twenty-third Psalm describes a substitute king.[27] Among other things, this short psalm has Word Links to four of the six occurrences of the word התמורה, which means "substitute" or "exchange." Such a thing cannot be coincidental. Psalm 23 contains this anagram of Jozadak: "He leads me in right paths [Jozadak BA] for his name's sake" (Ps 23:3). The "right path" could refer to the substitute's march down the city of Babylon's Processional Way, braving jeering crowds as he went. A Proverbs verse makes the same association ("I have led you in the paths [Jozadak BA] of uprightness" Prov 4:11). Another Jozadak anagram in Psalms joins "paths" and the התמורה clue. Psalm 17:5 says, "My steps have held fast to your paths [Jozadak BA]; my feet have not slipped." The two adjacent words "paths" and "my feet" between them contain the letters of התמורה, which means "substitute." Finally, the author of Neh 5:17, writing more than a century after Jozadak's execution, says, "There were at my table one hundred fifty [Messiah BA] people, Jews and officials, besides those who came to us from the nations around [Jozadak, Baruch BAs] us." The missing fact is that each substitute king hosted sumptuous banquets each evening of his short life. In this context, "messiah" means "anointed." The Baruch BA suggests that he, too, was captured at Jerusalem, and might also have died as a replacement king.

Nebuchadnezzar would have executed Jozadak sometime in the 560s. (Eleven eclipses darkened the sun or moon over Babylon between 569 and late 562 when the great king's reign ended, and we estimate that nine of them bought a substitute to the throne.[28]) Substitute kings received royal funerals and interments, and this famous line seems to express Jozadak's wish that he be buried in Jerusalem: "A day in your courts [Jozadak BA] is better than a thousand elsewhere. I would rather be a

27. See Kavanagh, *Secrets*, 90–92.

28. See Kudlek and Mickler, *Eclipses*, for dates and times. The estimate of nine substitutes in eleven eclipses is based upon eclipse shadings and which planets were visible during eclipses. Nine of eleven is unusual. Of the sixty-one eclipses over Babylon during the Jewish Exile, this author estimates that twenty-seven (44 percent) triggered enthronements. The ratio that the Nineveh letters show for Assyrian replacements is 50 percent. Over a longer period, the Babylonians would have seated a substitute king about every two years.

doorkeeper in the house of my God than live in the tents of wickedness" (Ps 84:10 [Heb 11]). The text has "Jacob" close by, so this may be the work of Second Isaiah. And here is the epitaph for the three who led the 570 revolt: "Those who are wise shall shine like the brightness of the sky, and those who lead many to righteousness [Jozadak, Jacob, Ezra BAs], like the stars forever and ever" (Dan 12:3).

Chapters 2 and 3 have featured biblical anagrams and demonstrated how they can open texts to our understanding. The next chapter, by concentrating on coded spellings, will answer a question that has stumped scholars for seventy years. The question is: Who is responsible for assembling the Deuteronomistic History?

4

The Dtr Solution: Shaphan and His Group

In 1943, Martin Noth advanced the theory that the books from Deuteronomy through Second Kings were the work of a single author who drew upon older sources and wrote during the exilic period.[1] With slight modification (many agree with Frank Cross that there was a pre-exilic edition), this view is now widely accepted among scholars. According to the *ABD*, "to the extent that any position in biblical studies can be regarded as the consensus viewpoint, the existence of the DH [Deuteronomistic History] has achieved almost canonical status."[2] Noth termed this individual "Dtr," an abbreviation for the person who compiled this extensive work.

According to Noth, the law as formed in Deut 4:44—30:20 was taken over by Dtr and applied in the balance of the history.[3] Scholars think that these chapters form the core of the "book of the law," which was ostensibly discovered by workmen repairing the temple in King Josiah's eighteenth year (622/621 BCE). The description, thrilling in itself and written by a master, is worth quoting: "The high priest Hilkiah said to Shaphan the secretary, 'I have found the book of the law in the house of the LORD.' When Hilkiah gave the book to Shaphan, he read it. Then Shaphan the

---

1. Nicholson in foreword to Noth, *Deuteronomistic History*, 10.
2. McKenzie, "Deuteronomistic History," 160–61.
3. Noth, *Deuteronomistic History*, 31.

The Shaphan Group

secretary came to the king, and reported to the king... 'The priest Hilkiah has given me a book.' Shaphan then read it aloud to the king. When the king heard the words of the book of the law, he tore his clothes" (2 Kgs 22:8–11). Reform quickly followed repentance. After the people themselves heard the book's words, they celebrated Passover and joined in a covenant ceremony. Josiah's officials demolished the high places sacred to other gods and centralized worship of the Lord at the Jerusalem temple. It was a heady time.

Where did this "book of the law" originate? Who wrote it?

Because the book was found in King Josiah's time, an obvious place to begin the search was with people of prominence who had lived toward the end of the seventh century. This is far from an original idea. Moshe Weinfeld, who wrote feature articles on Deuteronomy in both *EncJud* and *ABD*, notes a prominent view that "the Deuteronomist, the editor of Joshua–Kings, and the editor of the prose sermons in Jeremiah are products of a continuous literary school starting in the middle of the seventh century and ending somewhere in the middle of the sixth century."[4] Based upon a knowledge of coding and probabilities, this author decided to join in the search for Dtr.

A previous book had charted significant coding of three dozen names throughout Hebrew Scripture.[5] These were narrowed to notables who worked during the Exile. They were the prodigy Daniel; Jeremiah the prophet; Baruch, Jeremiah's accomplished scribe; Jacob, who was Second Isaiah; and the P Source Ezra. Jozadak, Ezra's brother and his rival for the high priesthood, also joined the list. That brought the exilic total to six. Fortunately, for all but Jozadak, some of the labor of calibrating anagrams and coding had already been completed. The other group of Dtr candidates centered upon Shaphan, King Josiah's Secretary, who had figured prominently in the book-of-the-law discovery. For search purposes, alongside him were his father Azaliah; Shaphan's sons Elasah, Gemariah, and Ahikam; Micaiah and his son Achbor—courtiers of Josiah;[6] Asaiah, who held the title of King's Servant to Josiah; and Huldah the prophetess, who had been consulted about the newly found Deuteronomy scroll.

---

4. Weinfeld, *EncJud* 5:1582.

5. Kavanagh, *Exilic Code*, Appendix 4, 221.

6. There may have been two Micaiahs in Josiah's time. See Fretz, "Micaiah," 810–11. Coding searches have tested both alternates.

The Shaphan Group in King Josiah's Time
620 BCE

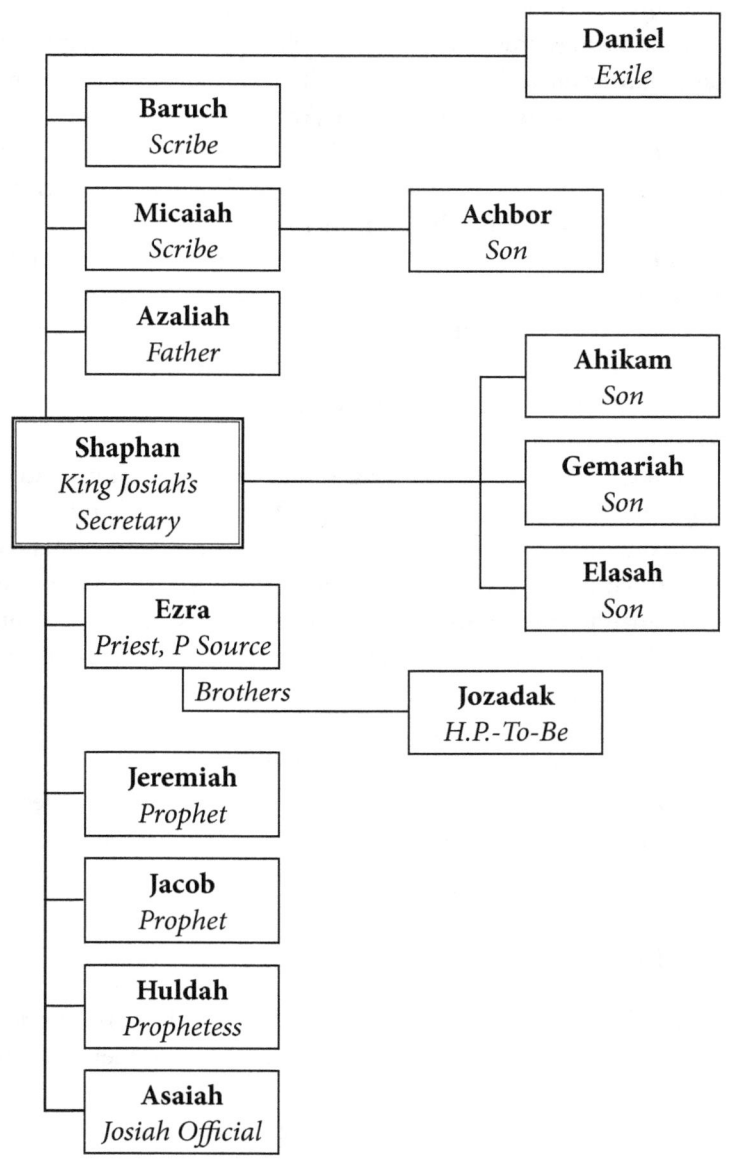

The Shaphan Group

Summarizing, in the exilic group were Daniel, Jeremiah, Baruch, Jacob, Ezra, and Jozadak, while the later-monarchy candidates for Dtr were Shaphan, Azaliah, Gemariah, Elasah, Ahikam, Micaiah, Achbor, Asaiah, and Huldah. Except for Daniel, any of the Dtr candidates might have worked during both the later monarchy and the Exile.

Rather than confining the search for Dtr to the books of Deuteronomy through Second Kings, this writer tested all of Scripture's 929 chapters for statistically significant coded spellings of the names of the fifteen candidates. When seeking coded spellings, one always worked with more than one version of a name. For example, for Ezra, the variations were "Ezra," "Ezra-son-of-Seraiah" (with two spellings of "Seraiah"), "Ezra-the-scribe," "Ezra-the-priest," and "Ezra-priest-the-scribe." For Asaiah, it was "Asaiah" and "Asaiah-servant-the-king." Athbash produced twenty-two different spellings for every name variation. Although the multiplication is simple, the total mounts quickly: 15 names × 22 athbash spellings × at least 4 name variations × 929 chapters = 1.2 million different searches. Only fast computers with clear instructions (that took years to refine) could execute such an effort.

Probability helps identify messages that biblical authors had intentionally concealed within their writings. The search program uses a threshold of one-in-a-thousand (.001) to exclude all but exceptional concentrations of coded spellings. This meant that there must be no more than one chance in one thousand that the result was *not* coincidental. A chapter's text words make up the numerator, while the balance of Scripture's text words form the denominator; the other proportion for the chi-square test has the chapter's coded spellings as the numerator while coded spellings in the rest of Scripture form the denominator. Thus, we are comparing ratios, a process that equalizes results between shorter and longer chapters. The two proportions must always be independent of each other.

Genesis 1 Introduces Shaphan

An example follows of how probability highlights Shaphan. The reader is cautioned, however, that this illustration uses anagrams rather than coded spellings. Genesis 1 is perhaps the most famous chapter in Scripture. Who is not familiar with "In the beginning God created the heavens

The Dtr Solution: Shaphan and His Group

and the earth"?[7] Scholars attribute to the P Source chapter 1 and the first four verses of chapter 2. Within Gen 1:1—2:4a are concealed eighty-two Shaphan anagrams. In a previous chapter, this writer nominated Ezra as P, while specifically excluding the Genesis passages from Ezra's work. Because of its anagrams, Gen 1:1—2:4a might be the work of someone named Shaphan, and there was only one Shaphan in Scripture. He is King Josiah's Secretary and happens to be one of our Dtr candidates. However, a sizable group of anagrams does not guarantee authorship, let alone *sole* authorship. The highlighted person might be one of the author's subjects, or perhaps have helped to write the chapter. Also, Scripture contains over a thousand Hebrew personal names, while Gen 1 has been tested for only a small number of them. And besides, we do not yet even know whether eighty-two anagrams is statistically significant to the .001 level.

Actually, it *is* significant, highly so. Eight-two Shaphan anagrams lie hidden among the text's 480 words. For comparison, computers give us the exact number of Shaphan anagrams in Scripture's remaining words. A chi-square analysis tells us that there is only a .000034 probability that such a number of anagrams could appear coincidentally in the Gen 1:1—2:4a text.[8] Put another way, there is but one chance in 29,000 that the Genesis concentration is due to coincidence alone. Given that level of significance, Shaphan might also be our Genesis P Source. The answer appears to be that, in part, he could be. Genesis chapters 1, 5, 6, 10, 11, 17, 23, and 35 are attributed to P. Half of these—chapters 1, 10, 23, and 35—contain significant Shaphan anagrams or coding, and may be from his hand.

Genesis 1:4 shows how the author applied the Shaphan anagrams. The letters used in the anagrams are underlined. "And God saw that the light [הָאוֹר] was good [טוֹב]; and God separated the light [הָאוֹר] from the darkness." And verse 1:20 weaves four different anagrams into the text: "And God said [וַיֹּאמֶר], 'Let the waters bring forth swarms of living

---

7. The author well remembers the forbearance Mr. Stine showed as he guided his beginning Hebrew students through this text on hot New Jersey days in the summer of 1958.

8. The chi-square proportions are 82 / 31,896 and 480 / 305,016. $P = 3.42 \times 10^{-5}$. The first proportion consists of Shaphan anagrams in Gen 1:1—2:4 and in the balance of Scripture, while the second has the same categories for text words.

creatures [נפש], and let birds fly above the earth [הארץ] across [פני] the dome of the sky.'"

Table 4.1 shows the word-by-word location of the eighty-two Shaphan anagrams in the Genesis text. One is "Shaphan" (שפן) itself and the others are athbash variants. The table not only enables experts to verify anagrams' placement and totals, but it also allows more casual readers to see how widely the author spread the Shaphan anagrams across his text. Although verse numbers were added well after Genesis was written, they still provide a useful measure of breadth. Thirty-five of the thirty-seven verses contain anagrams. This dispersion argues that Shaphan is the (or an) author rather than a subject featured in a smaller section of the Genesis passage.

TABLE 4.1
Shaphan Anagrams in Genesis 1:1—2:4

Anagram	Total	Chapter: Verse-Word
בוט	7	1:4-6, 10-12, 12-18, 18-12, 21-23, 25-18, 31-8
הארּ	29	1:1-7; 2-1; 4-4, 10; 9-10; 11-4, 18; 12-2; 15-5, 7; 16-5, 8, 13; 17-6, 8; 18-6; 20-11; 24-4; 25-5; 26-14, 19; 28-11, 22; 29-15; 30-3, 10; 2:1-3; 4-4, 5
וים	34	1:3-1; 5-4, 12; 6-1; 8-9; 9-1; 11-1, 13; 12-7, 14; 13-5, 14-1, 9, 14, 15, 16; 16-11, 18; 18-2; 19-5; 20-1; 21-19; 23-5; 24-1; 25-14; 26-1; 28-4; 29-1; 31-14; 2:2-3, 9; 3-4; 4-6, 11
ינפ	4	1:2-7, 13; 20-13; 29-13
לעק	3	1:7-10, 15; 8-3
רבי	1	2:4-5
שפן	4	1:20-6, 21-8, 24-5, 30:13
All	82	1:1-7; 2-1, 7, 13; 3-1; 4-4, 6, 10; 5-4, 12; 6-1; 7-10, 15; 8-3, 9; 9-1, 10; 10-12; 11:1, 4, 13, 18; 12:2, 7, 14, 18; 13-5; 14:1, 9, 14, 15, 16; 15-5, 7; 16-5, 8, 11, 13, 18; 17-6, 8; 18:2, 6, 12; 19-5; 20:1, 6, 11, 13; 21-8, 19, 23; 23-5; 24-1, 4, 5; 25-5, 14, 18; 26-1, 14, 19; 28-4, 11, 22; 29-1, 13, 15; 30-3, 10, 13; 31-8, 14; 2:1-3; 2-3, 9; 3-4; 4-4, 5(2), 6, 11

The Dtr Solution: Shaphan and His Group

One problem encountered when working with coded spellings is that there is a deluge of data. Narrowing the field to fifteen later monarchy-exilic personages offered some relief, but still not enough. Most of the fifteen names had two or three variations, four had four (Achbor, Huldah, Baruch, and Jacob), and Ezra used five. With seventeen, Daniel was an outlier. The more variations one tries, the more answers one will get. Some will be grounded in the original text's intentional coding, but the risk is that numerous others will be coincidental. We pass this lesson on to readers who may soon be doing their own decoding and further suggest making the number and nature of words tested appropriate to the object sought—as we had not previously done. To move forward, we pared the variants allowed to two per name for each of the fifteen. Typically, they were similar to "Achbor" and "Achbor-son-Micaiah." In Daniel's case, they were "Daniel" (דניאל, the five-letter version) and "Daniel-eunuch." Eunuch was used because the name of Daniel's father is not in Scripture.

Authors of the History

Based upon two variants apiece, Table 4.2 on the following page shows coded participation for fifteen notables in the Deuteronomistic corpus, which consists of the seven consecutive books from Deuteronomy through Second Kings.

Table 4.2 employs percentages so that readers can more easily draw comparisons among the fifteen later monarchy and exilic notables. The percentages deal with numbers of chapters that contain at least one statistically significant set of coded spellings. Looking at the first number (62%), Shaphan's father Azaliah had coded spellings of either or both "Azaliah" and "Azaliah son of Meshullam" in twenty-one of Deuteronomy's thirty-four chapters (21 / 34 = 62%). Like others listed in the table's left-hand column, only two coded variations of the name Azaliah could be counted. These usually were the given name and that same name with a parent ("Elasah son of Shaphan") or an occupation, like "Baruch the scribe" or "Huldah the prophetess." The table shades percentages at or above 73 percent, to identify higher levels of participation. But the shading should not obscure a surprising fact: almost all of the fifteen significantly encoded their signatures in at least six out of ten of the chapters ascribed to Dtr. The figures are strong, and they are broadly based.

The Shaphan Group

TABLE 4.2
Percent of DH Chapters Coded with Names
of 15 Notables from Later Monarchy and Exile

	Deut	Josh	Judg	Sam	Kgs	Overall
Chapters	34	24	21	55	47	181
Azaliah father of Shaphan	62%	88%	86%	71%	72%	73%
Shaphan son of Azaliah	47	83	76	65	83	70
Gemariah son of Shaphan	53	79	71	60	64	64
Ahikam son of Shaphan	56	83	48	49	72	61
Elasah son of Shaphan	74	75	67	60	68	67
Micaiah the scribe	85	96	95	64	60	75
Achbor son of Micaiah	65	88	71	65	74	71
Asaiah servant of the king	47	54	33	22	26	33
Huldah the prophetess	44	83	86	53	57	60
Jeremiah the prophet	65	83	71	75	77	74
Baruch the scribe	50	96	86	47	47	53
Ezra the P Source	79	75	67	65	66	70
Jacob Second Isaiah	74	88	71	60	77	72
Jozadak Ezra's brother	53	75	81	60	66	65
Daniel	71	88	76	69	57	70
Average percent	62%	82%	72%	59%	64%	66%

Before proceeding, however, here is a caveat. By its very nature, the data contains an unknown portion of coincidental spellings that pile atop the intended coding and inflate the percentages by some amount. Limiting spelling variations to two per historical person helps some, but cannot wholly rid us of "naturally" occurring coded spellings. At chapter's end we shall recommend a further adjustment. In the interim, readers can have confidence in the direction, if not the precise magnitude of the percentages, that the table shows. Taking that into account, some highlights are listed below.

The Dtr Solution: Shaphan and His Group

- Joshua is easily the most heavily coded book in the DH. Baruch and Micaiah have significant coding in twenty-three of the twenty-four chapters, while Azaliah, Achbor, and Jacob (Second Isaiah) are close behind.
- The combined Samuel books are the most lightly coded—probably because much of their material predates the DH—but even in Samuel, most notables have significant signatures in at least 60 percent of the chapters.
- Micaiah the scribe has the heaviest coding in Deuteronomy, Joshua, and Judges; Jeremiah leads in Samuel; and Shaphan contributes the most to Kings.
- Over the entire DH, Micaiah, Jeremiah, and Shaphan's father Azaliah rank the highest in proportions of chapters with coded signatures.
- Shaphan, Achbor, Ezra, Jacob, and Daniel are close behind Micaiah, Jeremiah, and Azaliah—the three leaders.

Table 4.2 makes obvious what to this writer comes as a complete surprise. The Shaphan group worked closely with the prophets and priests of those times—Huldah, Jeremiah, and Jacob—as well as the priestly brothers Ezra and Jozadak. In turn, those individuals worked upon Scripture with each other, while operating in company with those who staffed the Shaphan workshop. Comparing the percentages of Baruch and Jeremiah indicates that the two did not always work as a team. Baruch excelled in composing Joshua and Judges, while Jeremiah led in Samuel and Kings. Although coded names generally indicate that the person is either a subject or an author of the piece, it is doubtful that Micaiah or Achbor would have been newsmakers during the later monarchy. Probably in every case but one we should be thinking of authorship.

That one exception is Daniel. Scripture says that in the third year of Jehoiakim (603 BCE) the Babylonians took the "youth" Daniel from Judah and then raised him in Nebuchadnezzar's court. Eighteen years prior to that, in 621, workmen found the scroll that scholars think contained many chapters from the book of Deuteronomy,[9] some of which also contained "Daniel" coded spellings. If the scroll did indeed consist of Deuteronomy materials with significant Daniel signatures, we have a problem. In 621,

9. Althann, "Josiah," 1016.

when the book was "found," Daniel would scarcely have been born. An answer to that is that the newly found scroll was not a portion of Deuteronomy but rather a text by young Jeremiah. Elsewhere this author has written that in 2 Chr 34, which relates the story of the scroll, "Jeremiah's book of the law" (ספרהתורהלירמיהו) is encoded *ninety-nine times*.[10] Whether that original text survives is an open question, but it certainly need not be the current Deuteronomy with its heavier Daniel coding.

"Daniel," at 88 percent, has an exceptional coding score in Joshua, and another percentage in Judges that is above average. These suggest that he worked as a colleague with Jacob, Micaiah, Baruch, and the rest during composition. While such speculation is a lot to load upon a newly conceived measurement system, it probably means that Daniel was in the west—not in Babylon—when the Dtr group wrote those two books. Scripture tells us that Jeremiah and Baruch evaded the 587/586 exile of their fellow Judahites, and it is reasonable that others in the Shaphan group received the same protection that King Nebuchadnezzar extended to the testy prophet (see Jer 39).

The coding for the priest Jozadak is similar to that for Daniel: high in Joshua and Judges and lower in the rest of the DH books. First Chronicles 6:15 says that Jozadak (also spelled Jehozadak) went to Babylon after Jerusalem's fall, so he might have returned to Palestine or Egypt when Daniel did. All in all, however, we need to become far more proficient in decoding, anagrams, and Word Links before we are able to confirm such things.

Huldah's Mastery of Coding

We should go no further before remarking on the quality of the coding of the prophetess Huldah, the lone woman in the group of fifteen. To reduce the number of "Huldah" variants to two, we reluctantly parted with "Huldah-wife-Shallum," which had produced many cleverly wrought coded spellings in Deuteronomy and elsewhere. The search list retained "Huldah-prophetess" along with "Huldah." This multi-name experiment showed that she wrote no small amount of Scripture, doing it with ingenuity and a touch that arguably exceeded all others. And the others in that group included masters like Jeremiah, Shaphan, Second Isaiah, and Ezra—fast company indeed.

10. Kavanagh, *Exilic Code*, 152.

The Dtr Solution: Shaphan and His Group

Table 4.3 gives readers a glimpse of Huldah's mastery of the coding art. Only examples from Deuteronomy are shown. The second column gives the English translation of the Hebrew, and the next shows the athbash scrambling of the true spelling. For example, the first item is from Deut 1, where she or a workmate spelled a strange group of letters four times, taking one letter per text word to form רבעפפמכלכבנ, which is an athbash of חלדהההאשׁתשׁלם, "Huldah the wife of Shallum."[11] That particular athbash is spelled in the remainder of Scripture only 222 other times, and the probability of finding four such spellings in a text the size of Deut 1 is essentially zero. The table's other examples of Huldah's coding insertions also are quite rare.

TABLE 4.3
Examples of Huldah's Coding Expertise in Deuteronomy

Deut	English	Athbash	Spellings	Rest OT
1	HuldahWifeShallum	רבעפפמכלכבנ	4	222
6	HuldahWifeShallum	קסאתתדוהוסן	2	147
7	HuldahWifeShallum	זגבייינעסעגב	1	11
8	HuldahWifeShallum	פשררבדגדמל	4	463
12	HuldahProphetess	נציכברחעזך	2	127
14	HuldahWifeShallum	בורששפסעסוז	3	44
16	HuldahProphetess	וינבגלתחשׁג	2	128
16	HuldahWifeShallum	תדצקקסמנמד	2	86
18	HuldahWifeShallum	נציככזהוהץ	2	71
28	HuldahWifeShallum	סככצתבאבכי	5	175
30	Huldah	סבקץ	1	64
32	HuldahProphetess	מטפעעזקכברע	1	12

11. The four Deut 1 spellings start at verse 7, words 4, 7, 8, and 9. They end at 7-14, 17, 18, and 19. To test the first spelling, write רבעפפמכלכבנ across the top of a sheet and number from 7-4 through 7-14 down the left-hand margin. Next, make a check mark under each letter that text word 7-4 contains (it has only ב) and work your way though the following text words. Then circle the checks that will complete the coded spelling. When finished, you have an encoding in the sequence ברמלככבבפנ. Having seen how this works, you can leave future searches up to your computer.

The Shaphan Group

Before proceeding to the next phase of the Dtr search, consider Daniel. According to coding evidence, Daniel was a real person. Thousands of statistically significant encodings of Daniel are spread across Hebrew Scripture—material that will soon be available to scholars who may want to address the authenticity problem. An expert on the book of Daniel has concluded, "Daniel is not a historical person but a figure of legend."[12] However, scholars may wish to reconsider that finding in light of this fresh anagram and coding evidence.

Shaphan's Leadership

How many people worked to produce the DH? Judging by the information in Table 4.3, fourteen of the fifteen (excluding only Asaiah) did so, though participation in different books varied. On individual chapters, it is not uncommon to find ten or even a dozen different names with coding of significance, and several DH chapters (Josh 15; Judg 12; 1 Kgs 6, 7) conceal coded spellings of all fifteen. But how could a committee, as it were, have composed something as compelling as Deuteronomy, as diverse as Judges, as methodical as Kings? It may be that a leader such as Jacob, Jeremiah, or Shaphan set the style for a book or a group of chapters within it. Imagine the task of encoding a hundred sets of names (each with perhaps a dozen spellings), adding anagrams to the mix, and all the while selecting vocabulary that established Word Links with other Scripture! The interplay between priests, prophets, and scribes must have been something to behold. Also, did the group complete Joshua before beginning Judges? Does the actual sequence within the DH match what we have now? Did those in Babylon or Egypt use Scripture to communicate with the Jerusalem center? Did different workshops in Babylon, Israel, or Egypt compose portions of the same book? Should we not be thinking in terms of chapters rather than of books? There must have been connections between political events and composition. Certainly some DH chapters came into being in response to occurrences in Judah or elsewhere.

Because we are examining the labor of at least a dozen people over many decades, it is difficult to define who Dtr was. And beyond the Shaphan family and the prophets-priests group there are certainly oth-

12. Collins, "Daniel," 30.

ers who contributed to the Deuteronomistic History. There probably were five or ten and perhaps even more. As students of Scripture join the search, they are bound to discover additional authors and scribes who helped to shape this part of the Bible. While the fifteen already identified should be thought of as the Dtr, but for a time let us focus upon Shaphan himself.

Deuteronomy 11 is a pristine example of Dtr's writing, and Shaphan has significant coding within it. In 11:13–15, he or another writer spelled out an unusual athbash version of "Shaphan son of Azaliah" three consecutive times, and added three Shaphan anagrams for good measure.[13] That passage says: "If you will only heed his every commandment [Shaphan BA] that I am commanding you today [Shaphan BA]—loving the LORD your God, and serving him with all your heart and with all your soul [Shaphan BA]— then he will give the rain for your land in its season, the early rain and the later rain, and you will gather in your grain, your wine, and your oil; and he will give grass in your fields . . ." (Deut 11:13–15). Coding in these verses carries more statistical weight than the three anagrams.

One of the verses from the same chapter that relies only upon anagrams to announce Shaphan's presence says: ". . . then the LORD will drive out all these nations [Shaphan BA] before you [two different Shaphan BAs], and you will dispossess [Shaphan BA] nations [Shaphan BA] larger and mightier [Shaphan BA] than yourselves" (Deut 11:23). After these illustrations, consider Shaphan anagrams across the expanse of Deut 4:44—30:20, which some think was "the book of the law." Those chapters contain 912 Shaphan anagrams, and the probability of finding so many is essentially zero.[14] Shaphan, the Secretary to King Josiah, might be our chief Deuteronomistic Historian. At the very least, he collaborated in a considerable portion of the book of Deuteronomy, and often when he did so, Shaphan employed anagrams instead of coded spellings.

The shading in table 4.2 shows that the workhorses in Deuteronomy's composition were Shaphan's father Azaliah, Shaphan's three sons, and

---

13. The unusual athbash spelling of שפנבנאצליהו is גשצוצההתעטי. The first spelling starts at v 13, word 20, and ends at 14-10; the second and third spellings begin at 14-1 and 14-2 and end at 15-1 and 15-2, respectively. The probability of coincidence is 9.75×10^{-14}.

14. The chi-square proportions are 912 / 10,234 and 31,066 / 295,262. $P = 2.12 \times 10^{-6}$. The first proportion consists of Shaphan anagrams and text words in Deut 4:44—30:20; the second has the same categories in the rest of Scripture.

The Shaphan Group

Micaiah and his child Achbor. Micaiah "signed" twenty-nine chapters, while Ezra and Jacob had over two dozen apiece. Jeremiah has long been high on scholars' lists of Dtr suspects. He has significant coded spellings in no fewer than seventeen chapters within the book-of-the-law core and in Deut 1, 3, and 31–33 outside of it. (Interestingly, in eleven of his seventeen Deuteronomy chapters, Jeremiah shares composition with his assistant Baruch. This is perhaps a lesser number than one might expect.) The Micaiah encoded in Deuteronomy could have been the father of Achbor (2 Kgs 22:12). Achbor, with Shaphan and others, was a member of the delegation sent to consult the prophetess Huldah about the newly discovered book of the law (2 Kgs 22:12–14).[15]

However, Micaiah was also the name of Shaphan's grandson. To the extent that the book of the law was a seventh-century creation, the grandson could not have written it, because there is strong evidence—now to be introduced—that Shaphan, when he served King Josiah, would have been too young to be a grandfather. First, Shaphan wrote Ps 90, which indicates that he survived terrible times while living into his eighties. We quote some of the psalm below:

> A prayer of Moses, the man of God . . . A thousand years in your sight are like [Shaphan BA] . . . a watch [Shaphan BA] in the night . . . For we are consumed by your anger; by your wrath we are overwhelmed . . . For all our days [Shaphan BA] pass away under your wrath; our years come to an end like a sigh. The days of our life are seventy years, *or perhaps eighty* [Shaphan BA, emphasis added], if we are strong [Shaphan BA]; even then their span is only toil and trouble; they are soon gone, and we fly away. Who considers the power of your anger? Your wrath is as great as the fear that is due you . . . Turn, O LORD! How long? Have compassion on your servants! Satisfy us with your steadfast love [חסדך, two Shaphan BAs] . . . (Ps 90:1, 4, 7, 9–11, 13–14).

Two of the less usual athbash spellings of "Shaphan" are בתד and הבס. Psalm 90's חסדך, which is translated as "your steadfast love," contains the letters of both. These and the other anagrams mark Shaphan as either the subject or author of this psalm, with author by far the most likely.

"We are consumed by your anger; by your wrath we are overwhelmed," writes the psalmist Shaphan. "For all our days pass away under your wrath . . . Your wrath is as great as the fear that is due you" (Ps 90:7, 9,

---

15. The prophetess Huldah had significant coding in Deut 20, 27, and 33.

11). And what generation of Israelites felt more of the wrath of God than Shaphan's? As one in a high position, he had initiated and then helped to carry through Josiah's reforms of covenant, priesthood, Scripture, and worship. Shaphan had been young, devoted, accomplished, and impassioned. But then his reformer king died in battle, and Judah fell under Egyptian and then Babylonian control. A welter of new rulers and forced exiles filled the next several decades. In 587, when Nebuchadnezzar besieged and then razed Judah's cities, Shaphan was an eyewitness to the extinction of Israel's national life. Slaughter and destruction were everywhere. The Babylonians cut off David's dynasty, leveled Solomon's temple, and seized the Promised Land. Nebuchadnezzar killed or exiled the Judahite elite, though Jeremiah and others like Shaphan were spared deportation. Shaphan's hopes must have soared when the Babylonians named his grandson Gedaliah the governor of Judah. But those hopes would have been quickly dashed when the new governor was assassinated by an agent of neighboring Ammon.

A reconstruction of what may have happened next is set forth below. After Gedaliah's murder, Shaphan joined other Judahites in seeking refuge in Egypt. With help from Jewish refugees, Pharaoh fought off at least one further Babylonian expedition, though it could have been a near thing. Finally, in the early 570s, the Egyptian Israelites assembled their own forces, left Egypt, hired Cyrus, and proceeded northward. At this point, Daniel and Jozadak may have traveled from Babylon to join their western comrades. After early successes against Moab, Philistia, and other neighboring countries, the Judahites retook Jerusalem. Responding, authorities took revenge against Jewish exiles in Babylonia. Some were killed outright and others were imprisoned. (The term "plague" in Scripture may refer to this.) While this repression was still under way, Nebuchadnezzar marched to Palestine, crushed the rebellion, and retook Jerusalem. Another possibility is that a neighbor such as Moab may have won that victory and then traded its captives to the Babylonians. Afterward, authorities put Ezekiel to death as a substitute king of Babylon, though before dying the prophet obtained release of Jehoiachin, Daniel, and other rebels.

This, or something reasonably close to it, is what Shaphan looked back upon when he wrote in Ps 90, "We are consumed by your anger; by your wrath we are overwhelmed." During most of Shaphan's lifetime, disaster had followed disaster; God's wrath must have seemed unremitting.

The Shaphan Group

Can we fix the date of Ps 90? In it the author wrote, "The days of our life are seventy years, or perhaps eighty [Shaphan BA], if we are strong [Shaphan BA]." The anagrams testify that when Shaphan wrote the psalm he was at least eighty years old, and perhaps a few years beyond that. We know that Shaphan was the King's Secretary in the eighteenth year of Josiah's reign, the year when repairmen found the book of the law. By our calendar, this was during 622/621 BCE. If Shaphan was then twenty-five and, say, eighty years of age when he composed Ps 90, he wrote the psalm in 567 BCE, which is fifty-five years after 622. If he were older than twenty-five in 622, then the psalm's date moves backwards toward 570; if younger, the dating approaches 565. Psalm 90 ends on a peculiar note. Shaphan writes, "Let the favor of the LORD our God be upon us, and prosper for us the work of our hands—O prosper the work of our hands!" (Ps 90:17). While awaiting arrival of the Babylonian army, was he petitioning that Jerusalem's reconstructed defenses might survive the assault?

Slight adjustments of the date of Ps 90 are not important here. What matters is that Shaphan lived a very long life, during which he could have worked with several sets of contemporaries and produced a great deal of Hebrew Scripture. This discovery affects another matter. There is now no need to seek two Dtrs—one who lived during the later monarchy and a second who worked during the Exile. Shaphan and the group around him would have served as both.

Of the 150 psalms, only Ps 90 is attributed to Moses. We think that this is not by chance. Psalm 90 is biographical. Old Shaphan is attempting to interpret the ruin of his life's work in light of an omnipotent but furious God. But why introduce Moses? One might hazard that the Exodus saga of Moses leading the children of Israel from Egypt to the edge of the Promised Land disguised the exilic story of Shaphan at the head of a people bent upon liberating Judah. Remembering that Ezra is Aaron and that Second Isaiah is Jacob, Shaphan might be the stand-in for Moses. We shall return to the Shaphan-Moses question when we explore who wrote the first four books of Moses—Genesis through Numbers.

Shaphan as Qohelet

We now move to an entirely different piece of Scripture, the book of Ecclesiastes. Because of linguistic evidence and its unique pattern of thought, scholars generally agree that Ecclesiastes is a late book. After

The Dtr Solution: Shaphan and His Group

reviewing the literature, one expert says that "a date in the latter half of the third century is possible," while another writes that between 250 and 225 seems the "most likely" time of composition.[16] With considerably less analytical capability, I admit to sharing the view that Ecclesiastes was a late composition. However, a date at the end of the seventh century now appears conceivable. It would be more than three centuries earlier than previously thought. The reasons for considering such a shift are Shaphan anagrams and coding.

In Eccl 2–7, 9, and 11, the collective authors used statistically significant bunches of the Shaphan anagram בוט (switching the first and last letters produces "good"). Less frequently occurring athbash spellings of Shaphan are לעק and דחך. These confer Shaphan significance on Eccl 3 and 11. In fact, in Eccl 3, the author used five differently spelled anagrams.[17] That chapter's poem is often quoted:

> For everything there is a season, and a time for every matter under heaven . . . a time to be born, and a time to die; a time to plant, and a time to pluck up [Shaphan BA] what is planted . . . a time to tear [Shaphan BA], and a time to sew; a time to keep silence, and a time to speak . . . I know that there is nothing better [Shaphan BA] for them than to be happy and enjoy [Shaphan BA] themselves as long as they live; moreover, it is God's gift that all should eat and drink and take [Shaphan BA] pleasure [Shaphan BA] in all their toil. I know that whatever God does endures forever; nothing can be added to it, nor anything taken from [Baruch BA] it; God [Shaphan BA] has done this, so that all should stand in awe before him [*three* Shaphan BAs]. That which is, already has been; that which is to be, already is; and God [Shaphan BA] seeks out what has gone by (Eccl 3:1, 2, 7, 12–15).

The author of Eccl 3 also referenced Baruch. The writer made an infinitive of the verb "diminish," the only place in Scripture where this was done. The spelling is לגרע. The *lamed* addition makes this the only place in the Bible that the BA occurs. However, the eleven Shaphan anagrams overshadow that single Baruch BA, despite its rarity.

The following evidence about coded signatures adds to the possibility that Ecclesiastes is early rather than late. Chapters 9, 10, and 12 are alive with statistically significant groups of spellings for all fifteen mem-

---

16. Blank, "Ecclesiastes," 13; Crenshaw, "Ecclesiastes," 275.

17. The five different Shaphan anagrams used in Eccl 3 are בוט, האר, יום, ינף, and לעק.

bers of the Shaphan group.[18] Chapter 9, for instance, contains fifty-six high-probability groups that average over four spellings apiece. Although Jozadak and Daniel have but one of those groups, Shaphan has eight and one of his sons has six. The rest are broadly spread.

In all, Shaphan himself has significant anagrams or coded spellings in ten of Ecclesiastes' twelve chapters, the exceptions being chapters 1 and 8. Limiting encodings to those that pass our .001-probability barrier, eight chapters employ either numerous or cleverly worked spellings of "Shaphan," "Shaphan the scribe," or "Shaphan son of Azaliah."

There is another choice that could explain this coding. Perhaps Shaphan and the others of his time are but the subjects of the book of Ecclesiastes. The book, then, concerned them but was not written in the sixth century BCE. We would attribute the coding-anagram material about Shaphan and his exilic compatriots to the desire to memorialize great predecessors. In this view, the book of Ecclesiastes becomes a biography of Shaphan written much later to reflect upon that previously hidden history. A strong point of any case for circa 250 BCE has been that the text contains two Persian loan words (in Eccl 2:5 and 8:11). We now think, however, that Shaphan was in the company of Cyrus (and possibly of other Persian mercenaries) during the 570 revolt, which would have allowed Shaphan to acquire at least a smattering of Persian.

Qohelet is the supposed author of Ecclesiastes. Common experiences connect Qohelet with Shaphan. Both were old and reflecting upon their lives. Both had taught others—Shaphan was Josiah's scribe and certainly tutored his sons. He may also have schooled the young prophet Jeremiah, for high-probability signatures of both are in Gen 1. Qohelet experienced a siege (Eccl 9:14), and Shaphan endured several of them. Qohelet was "king over Israel in Jerusalem" (Eccl 1:12), and extraordinary though it may seem, Shaphan might also have ruled when the Israelites briefly held the city (circa 570). Further, the tale of Qohelet seems to contain many veiled references to substitute kings (Eccl 4:14–16; 7:21; 8:12, 13; 9:2; 10:7, 16, 20), and Shaphan, during his long lifetime, knew personally each of the Jewish substitutes whom the Babylonians executed.

"Besides being wise, the Teacher also taught the people knowledge, weighing and studying and arranging many proverbs." So says v 9 of the

18. Eccl 9 has a chi-square P value of 4.0×10^{-11}, chapter 10 of 9.8×10^{-6}, and chapter 12 of 2.9×10^{-17}. Each calculation includes a reduction for nonsense groups, to be outlined subsequently.

concluding chapter of Ecclesiastes. That fits what we know about Shaphan, because probabilities will show that he influenced much of Proverbs. An inordinate percentage of Scripture's high-value "Shaphan" coded spellings lies within that book.[19] To give another example, Shaphan himself might have been the "poor wise man" who, by his wisdom, delivered a besieged city (Eccl 9:14–15). It could have involved the surrender of Jerusalem to the Babylonians. Provocatively, strong and rare coded spellings of "Nebuchadnezzar" underlie the two preceding verses.[20] Whatever year Ecclesiastes was written, it appears to contain specifics about Shaphan's life.

Because the significant coding and anagrams are an immutable part of the text, it seems that one must choose one of the following alternatives: (a) decide that the system in this case is faulty, (b) view the coded insertions as naming contemporary or near-contemporary people, or (c) hold that this is an historical account of bygone figures. The faulty-system possibility will be addressed in the discussion of nonsense words. The previous paragraphs set out the case for (c), that Shaphan and the others are from an earlier time, recalled three hundred years later. This has much to commend it. Or is the answer (b), wherein Ecclesiastes is a contemporary seventh- or sixth-century account, about those whose names are concealed within the text?

The Nonsense Word Test

We close by describing a rigorous test of whether the search system for coded spellings is sound. Especially with the Dtr discoveries (and others soon to be described), this writer has been concerned that too many significant spellings were being found. To address this question, I fashioned ten sets of two nonsense words each, modeled upon the true pairs of Shaphan family names used in the Dtr search. The nonsense words contained the same mix of Hebrew letters as the Dtr search's true words. The

---

19. The chi-square proportions are 36 / 674 and 6,912 / 298,584. $P = 5.21 \times 10^{-7}$. The first proportion consists of Shaphan encodings in individual Proverbs chapters over those in the balance of Scripture, while the second has the same categories for text words.

20. Two spellings of "Nebuchadnezzar" using the rare athbash פוגנרהפחמן start at verse 12, words 8 and 21, in chapter 9 and end at words 12-17 and 13-7. Of course this passage could relate to an earlier occasion when Shaphan at Jerusalem negotiated the surrender of besieged Judahites to the Babylonian army.

made-up words ranged from three to eleven letters, with clusters in the areas of four-to-five and ten-to-eleven letters. Every letter in every word was randomly drawn except that the second word in each pair always repeated the first three, four, or five letters contained in that pair's initial word. This imitated true pairs like "Ezra" and "Ezra-the-scribe."

Twenty words might seem like too small a sample, but each single word was increased to twenty-two by the athbash inflation process. That completed, we had 440 nonsense words to run against the totality of Hebrew Scripture. The question to decide was this: Would the nonsense words generate as high a proportion of significant spellings across Scripture as had the Dtr search's true words? Lengthy computer runs found that the true words were far more efficient in converting spellings into statistically significant groups. Once we had the conversion rate for nonsense words, we could simply test each true group to see whether it bettered that rate. If the true word did, we assumed that it was not random. If the group of coded spellings that we had tested did not pass, we assumed that it was random and discarded it.[21] In total, we rejected almost six thousand groups, or 21 percent of those we had originally found.

Undoubtedly, we have rejected some coded spellings that biblical authors intentionally fashioned and retained a few that they did not. Nevertheless, we think that the search system described in this book is sound. A major portion of its random results have been squeezed out, and in our opinion the findings to come can be relied upon. This is timely, because the next chapter will survey the Shaphan group's impact upon a considerable portion of Hebrew Scripture.

---

21. Nonsense words had 206,919 spellings within statistically significant groups and 69,495,706 outside such groups in the rest of Scripture. The product is .002977, termed the "nonsense line." Any individual true groups which, despite having statistical significance, fell below that nonsense line were deemed to be random and were discarded. Twenty-one percent (5,966) of all Shaphan-related groups were treated in that manner.

5

The Shaphan Group's Prodigious Output

In the preceding chapter we learned that Shaphan, his family, and his colleagues wrote much of the Deuteronomistic History. Their coded fingerprints fill the books of Deuteronomy through Second Kings in the form of anagrams and hidden spellings. Shaphan, who was King Josiah's secretary and whose career spanned the later monarchy and much of the Exile, probably led the group. Also among those who operated together were Shaphan's three sons and his father; fellow-courtiers Asaiah, Micaiah, and Achbor; the prophets Huldah, Jeremiah, and Jacob; the brothers Jozadak and Ezra; the scribe Baruch; and probably Daniel.

In this chapter we shall establish that this same group of experts drafted a large amount of other Scripture, and we shall be specific about what that scripture was. Before we embark on that journey, however, here is a summary of discoveries about coded writing.

- Those who wrote Scripture used several techniques to convey information.
- Techniques include Word Links, anagrams, and coded spellings.
- Athbash multiplies ways to spell anagrams and coded spellings.
- Coded spellings use one letter per text word taken from consecutive words.
- Some coded spellings are coincidental, while others are intentional.

The Shaphan Group

- Nonsense words establish a base line that separates coincidental from intentional coding.

The nonsense-word approach measures conversions of individual coded spellings into statistically significant groups. Spellings generated from nonsense words have a lower conversion ratio than those derived from Shaphan-group spellings, and these can be significantly different. This new conversion technique, we suggest, can contribute to OT scholarship. The batch of randomly drawn nonsense words we shall use has been tailored to match the characteristics of the Shaphan-group names. Another group of true names (for example, eighth-century, Restoration, or priestly) might call for differently configured dummy words. The point is that scholars will be able to refine this approach to fit their particular needs.

Shaphan Group Edits DH, Pentateuch

To test Shaphan-group participation against nonsense words, we offer this first group of texts. Not surprisingly, they constitute the DH—the books from Deuteronomy through Second Kings. Showing percentages above the base line is new to readers, so we have also included the more familiar measure of whether or not the item satisfies a probability of coincidence that is below .001. (Occasionally, when data is scanty, a plus base line percentage can fail to satisfy that probability standard.)

TABLE 5.1

Coded Spellings:

The Shaphan Group's Impact on Deuteronomistic History

Books	± Base Line	Probability Satisfied?
Deuteronomy	+24%	Yes
Joshua	+83	Yes
Judges	+34	Yes
Samuel	+14	No
Kings	+34	Yes
Total DH	+28%	Yes

The Shaphan Group's Prodigious Output

A glance shows that the fifteen members of Shaphan's group dominated composition of the book of Joshua; made solid contributions to Deuteronomy, Judges, and Kings; and had a more modest influence upon Samuel. Samuel flunked its probability test despite being 14 percentage points over the nonsense base line. The explanation is that Samuel had a limited number of coded spellings, but the book's editors efficiently converted what spellings they made into statistically significant groups. Overall, the DH bested the nonsense conversion line by 28 percent, a margin that cannot be due solely to coincidence.

Before continuing with the DH, here are some parting thoughts on nonsense words. They teach us that a substantial proportion of true spellings occur naturally, which complicates our measuring task. Also, whenever numerous true spellings surface, many nonsense words will also present themselves. Although this is so, true words consistently have a numerical advantage. For example, Ps 51 is stuffed with significantly coded spellings.[1] For the Shaphan group alone, that short psalm houses 149 significant Shaphan-group batches while at the same time containing 120 nonsense clusters. Both are sizable. Still, the 149 true groups are considerably more than 120 made-up ones, and that difference can be readily measured.

The Shaphan group used editing to do most of its work on the seven-book DH. Not infrequently, however, its members drafted entire chapters of new text. These are best identified by counting significant signature groups within each chapter and then applying a chi-square test. Joshua had seven chapters that passed this rigorous test (Josh 12, 13, and 15–19); Judges had two (Judg 5 and 12); and First Kings one (1 Kgs 6). The material in the seven Joshua chapters had sufficient spill-over to push the entire book into the beyond-coincidence zone.

Table 5.2 on the next page helps to demonstrate just how difficult it must have been to encode multiple spellings of names within a Hebrew text. The table shows the coding in Judg 12, which tells of the judge Jephthah, inter-tribal battles, and the Shibboleth password. We selected Judg 12 simply because it was among the shortest of the DH chapters that the group composed. By happenstance, it contains statistically significant groups from fourteen of the Shaphan group's fifteen members. All but one of the chapter's spellings employs athbash, which encoders used to create

---

1. See Appendix 3 of Kavanagh, *Exilic Code*, which details hundreds of these spellings.

89

The Shaphan Group

multiple versions of the same name. Although at 223 Hebrew text words the chapter is short, into it the authors crowded 266 spellings of coded words ranging from four to twelve letters each. The writers fashioned twenty-nine different groups of such spellings, each of which passed a stringent probability test (and in turn the twenty-nine together passed the same type of test for chapters).[2] The Shaphan-group authors did all this while writing cogent accounts that, over two millennia later, we still find holy and marvelous.

TABLE 5.2
Significant Signature Spellings by the Shaphan Group within Judges 12

Names (/ = son of)	Hebrew Letters	Significant Groups	Signature Spellings
Achbor/Micaiah	12	1	8
Ahikam	5	1	2
Ahikam/Shaphan	11	1	11
Asaiah	4	1	36
Asaiah King's Servant	11	1	4
Azaliah	6	1	15
Baruch the Scribe	8	2	4, 3
Daniel	5	1	3
Ezra the Scribe	8	1	8
Gemariah/Shaphan	11	2	23, 23
Huldah	4	2	12, 4
Huldah Prophetess	10	2	4, 2
Jacob	4	1	1
Jacob/Shelomoth	11	2	4, 8
Jeremiah Prophet	11	2	10, 7
Jozadak	5	1	3
Jozadak/Seraiah	11	1	2
Micaiah	5	2	4, 6
Micaiah the Scribe	9	2	8, 9
Shaphan the Scribe	7	2	22, 20
Totals		29	266

2. Each of the twenty-nine groups was under the .001 chi-squared probability standard and, as a whole, the chapter stood at .00109.

The Shaphan Group's Prodigious Output

The Shaphan group also played a major role in assembling the first three books of Scripture. According to the evidence from coded spellings, those writers accounted for fourteen chapters, including six Exodus chapters (25–27 and 36–38) and eight in Leviticus (1, 3, 4, 6, 9, 12, 15, and 19). Previously we identified Ezra as the P Source and said that he is also one of the fifteen in Shaphan's group. Experts attribute to the P Source Exod 25–27 and 36–38, and we are here broadening authorship to others beside Ezra. In addition to him, authors of some or all of these Exodus P Source chapters include Achbor, Ahikam, Asaiah, Baruch, Daniel, Elasah, and Huldah. It seems that the Shaphan group also served as the P Source. If so, Shaphan-led writers also edited or composed substantial portions of Genesis and Exodus that our coded spellings approach is not picking up. Because chapters are the basic unit of this technique, it is not well suited for dealing with edited texts—such as those of the P Source—which have shorter passages inserted here and there. To address this, we could modify the design of coded spellings but, for this book at least, we shall stick with chapters as our basic unit. Please keep in mind, however, that results will be understated, and that Shaphan and his colleagues did more than we can immediately identify.

The opening chapters of Genesis offer a sharp lesson. In the preceding chapter we introduced Shaphan by detailing his extensive use of anagrams in Gen 1. There were sufficient anagrams, in fact, to produce a near-zero probability of coincidence. Yet the coded spellings approach found little in Genesis. The prior sketch of Shaphan anagrams in Genesis also rated chapters 10 (pre-history) and 35 (Jacob saga) as heavily salted with his anagrams, but coded spellings found nothing significant. Demonstrably, biblical authors had ways other than coded spellings to mark their work, and anagrams were among those ways.

We now move to the book of Numbers.

In parsing the book of Numbers, we followed the analyses of experts.[3] The second column of table 5.3 (see following), "Content," shows this, with the shaded sections indicating high statistical significance. The table uses coded spelling groups per thousand text words as a simple way to display coding density. Scripture as a whole averages seventy-two groups per thousand. For Numbers, eight of the opening chapters ("Preparations" at 104) and the book's final eleven ("Promised Land" at 92) are very high, while the "Camp Purity" and "Rebellions" chapters

---

3. See Milgrom, "Numbers," 1146–48.

The Shaphan Group

(Num 5–6, 11–14, and 16–17) seem to be holdovers without coding. The highly coded Preparations and Promised Land sections (Num 1–4, 7–10, and 26–36) could pertain to the 570s when the Cyrus-led rebellion was under way. Chapter 3 of this book describes what anagrams tell us about those years. Dividing Numbers into chapters featuring either laws or narratives shows that the Shaphan composers did more with legal chapters (91 per thousand) than with the narrative ones (68).

TABLE 5.3
Coded Spellings/Thousand Text Words:
The Shaphan Group's Impact on Sections in the Book of Numbers
(Shading Shows Statistical Significance)

Book of Numbers Chapters	Content of Sections	Spelling Groups/ Thousand	Probability Satisfied?
Scripture	All	72	
Numbers		68	No
1–4, 7–10	Preparations	104	Yes
5–6	Camp Purity	28	No
11–14, 16–17	Rebellions	32	No
26–36	Promised Land	92	Yes
20 law chapters	Laws	91	Yes
17 nar. chapters	Narratives	68	No

For scholarly purposes, however, this section-by-section approach to Numbers is short on details. As a remedy, table 5.4 gives a chapter-by-chapter listing of the signature groups per thousand words. Shaded chapters indicate chi-square coding that exceeds the .001 base line standard. For most chapters, a higher level of spellings produces a solid probability result. A notable exception is chapter 24, which carries a low 42 per thousand. It earns its shading because it contains six different high-probability groups of "Elasah," the name of one of Shaphan's sons. Almost half the chapter's coded groups had Elasah's signature. All in all, this proves the worth of chi-square testing in comparison to a different measure like spellings per thousand text words (S/1000 in table 5.4). The table shows that four other chapters (7, 10, 33, and 34) also conceal plenty of coded spellings. Including these, the Shaphan group, in part or whole, wrote chapters 1–3, 7, 10, 19, 24, 26, 28, 29, 33, 34, and 36. The table reveals that Num 1, with 588 signatures per thousand words, is in a class by itself. Certainly it is among the highest in all of Scripture. Ostensibly, the chapter is about Moses taking a census of Israel. In actuality, it must have served a more immediate exilic purpose, such as a count of the forces assembled in the 570s to take back the Promised Land.

TABLE 5.4
Coded Spellings/Thousand Text Words:
The Shaphan Group's Impact on Chapters in the Book of Numbers
(Shading Shows Statistical Significance)

C	S/1000	C	S/1000	C	S/1000	C	S/1000
1	588	10	91	19	118	28	114
2	284	11	16	20	17	29	240
3	110	12	25	21	17	30	42
4	49	13	48	22	11	31	38
5	28	14	17	23	28	32	68
6	28	15	31	24	42	33	93
7	92	16	24	25	22	34	109
8	52	17	73	26	117	35	25
9	59	18	12	27	41	36	203

To illustrate further, details follow about coding of the Shaphan group members. A dozen of the fifteen authors had a lot to do with the book of Numbers. Ranking serves only limited purpose since the coded spellings of each have essentially a zero percent probability of coincidence. Nevertheless, here they are. Micaiah, who was Shaphan's contemporary in Josiah's court, led all others with ninety-four coded groups. Shaphan and two of his sons, Gemariah and Elasah, followed Micaiah. Grouped in the high seventies were Daniel, Jeremiah, and the two priestly brothers Jozadak and Ezra, while Huldah, Jacob, Asaiah and three others were below that level.

At the bottom of the list of writers (or perhaps of subjects, since positive coding could signify either subject or author) is Shaphan's father Azaliah. If we are correct about a date of around 570 BCE for Numbers, Azaliah would have been dead for many years. Also at the bottom of the ranking list is Micaiah's son Achbor and Shaphan's son Ahikam. Though both led in drafting the history books, they seem to have played only a minor role in Numbers. All of this is preliminary, since Scripture contains some thirteen hundred Hebrew personal names and we are working with only a handful. Eventually, persistent scholars with all possibilities before them will perform a more comprehensive examination.

Disclosure of First Importance

This writer now presents a disclosure of first importance, one that could rival any ever made in the study of the Hebrew Bible. The Shaphan group wrote or strongly influenced a large amount of the Writings and of the Prophets. We draw this conclusion based upon clear—we think irrefutable—evidence of coded writing within Scripture. So far we have found that Shaphan and his colleagues edited the books from Deuteronomy through Second Kings, and that these same experts shaped portions of the Torah—Genesis, Exodus, and Numbers. Now we add this: these fifteen Judahites also wrote or influenced to a statistically significant degree the books of Joshua, Psalms, Proverbs, Job, Songs, Lamentations, and Daniel. Moreover, the Shaphan group initiated or heavily edited much of the Prophets, including the books of Isaiah, Hosea, Joel, Amos, Micah, Nahum, and Habakkuk. Finally, the names of the members of the Shaphan group are also significantly coded in the books of Ezra and Nehemiah. (Appendix 2 gives details of all these books.)

We came to form these startling conclusions by applying probabilities to coded writing, of which the basic unit of measurement is the statistically significant group. With rare letter combinations it can take only a single spelling to form a significant group, but with common letters it can require one hundred spellings or even more. Scripture-wide, the average number of hidden spellings necessary to achieve statistical significance is eleven.

The Shaphan Group Writes Psalms

A real-life example from Psalms follows. Hidden within Ps 1 are three coded spellings of חטמע, which is an athbash of "Huldah." In the rest of Scripture, that spelling occurs only 422 other times. Psalm 1 contains 67 text words, while the remainder of Scripture has 305,429. The two chi-square proportions are 3 / 422 and 67 / 305,429, and they yield a probability of coincidence of 1.21×10^{-20}. This decimal is well below our threshold of .001. The three Huldah spellings in Ps 1, then, qualify as a statistically significant group. We tested all of Scripture for coded spellings of "Huldah," "Huldah the prophetess," and athbash variants of the two, accumulating statistically significant groups as we went. We then repeated the process for the other members of Stephan's group. In total, the fifteen pairs of names produced 3,250 groups within Psalms, and 18,724 in the rest of Scripture. Knowing the exact numbers of text words in both, it was simple to test whether this could be coincidental. The calculation's result was 0. That is, the probability that a text the size of Psalms would contain that many coded groups by chance alone was simply zero. Common sense confirms this statistical conclusion: the book of Psalms, with 6 percent of the Bible's text words, has 15 percent of its Shaphan-related significant groups. Given that we are working with thousands of both text words and statistically significant groups, chance is out of the question. Only intent could have accomplished this.

There are numerous psalms. Does this zero probability of coincidence for the entire book mean that Shaphan-group members were involved in every psalm? No, but only nine psalms have a below-average number of significant groups; for all the others, the balance is well in favor of Shaphan-related coded spellings. Of the nine below-average psalms, two (Pss 118 and 134) have statistically significant numbers of "Baruch" biblical anagrams. A third, Ps 53, ends with the words "Jacob will rejoice; Israel will be glad"—a Jacob-Israel parallel that Second Isaiah used to sign his work. In summary, 144 psalms appear to be by or about the Shaphan group, and only Pss 28, 29, 33, 96, 100, and 115 do not, at present, qualify.

There is another, more stringent, way of deciding whether the Shaphan group authored any single psalm. Appendix 1 displays the results of this rigorous approach. Within the appendix are eighty-seven psalms that satisfy a probability standard of .001 (one chance in a thousand of being coincidental). Additionally, eleven psalms make the appendix by slightly relaxing that standard to .005 (one chance in five hundred). With the chi-square method, the total is either eighty-seven or ninety-eight psalms, depending upon where one draws the probability line. The larger number is about two-thirds of the 150 psalms. The above-average approach concluded that "144 psalms are by or about the Shaphan group," while appendix 1 offered either eighty-seven or ninety-eight psalms. Readers may take their choice (or make no choice at all). Whatever the total actually is, Shaphan and his colleagues were in good part responsible for the book of Psalms.

Did each of Shaphan's compatriots substantially contribute to the book of Psalms? The answer is a resounding yes. Each and every one of those fifteen Judahites had their names encoded within the psalm texts to a statistically lopsided extent. The proof is that not one of the fifteen chi-square results had fewer than fifty zeros to the right of the decimal point. (After four or five zeros, most would conclude that there is no real possibility of coincidence.) However, clearly all fifteen could not have written or been the subject of every psalm, so a psalm-by-psalm analysis remains to be made. As an aid to that, appendix 1 shows which Shaphan-group members have their names significantly encoded within ninety-eight of the psalms.

Other tests of the breadth of authorship within Psalms are easily done. Most psalms have headings, which range from one word to more than a dozen. Two examples are "To the leader. A Psalm of David" and "A Song. A Psalm of the Korahites." Over the centuries, psalm headings have drawn intense scholarly interest. Reasonably, those who study Scripture have suspected that the headings contained clues about dating and authorship. So far, however, no conclusions have emerged—until now, with the discovery of coded signatures. Probabilities tell us that all fifteen members of the Shaphan group made strong contributions to the book of Psalms. To see whether this held true in smaller lots, I used Nahum Sarna's categories to test psalms with Korah and Asaph headings, along with the so-called royal psalms.[4]

Using pairs of the Shaphan-group names and their athbash variants, I ran over six hundred name versions against the batches of Korah, Asaph, and royal psalms. I expected to find that some of the fifteen had

---

4. Sarna, "Psalms," 1310. "Korah" psalms were 42–49, 84, 85, 87, and 88; those with "Asaph" in the title were 50 and 73–83; royal psalms were 2, 18, 20, 21, 28, 44, 45, 61, 63, 72, 84, 89, 101, 110, and 132.

worked on one batch and others on another. Instead, the results were different. The name of almost every member of the Shaphan group was significantly coded in the Korah, Asaph, and royal batches of psalms. Of the forty-five trials (fifteen names times three psalm batches), forty-one had essentially no chance of coincidence. As to the four remaining, they recorded modest 4, 3, 3, and 2 percent chances of coincidence. Ezra, Shaphan, and Jeremiah had those lower scores, so they probably did not work on all of the Korah and Asaph psalms. (Chi-square results showed full participation in the royal psalms.)

Whoever assembled Psalms grouped them into five books. This, too, has been a subject of intense research for many a century. The thinking is that this five-part division is the product of "a long and complex history involving several small collections and their combination into larger units."[5] To see if the coded-writing discovery could shed any light on this aspect of psalm research, I ran the fifteen sets of Shaphan names against Book V of Psalms, which includes Pss 107–50. The outcome at least equaled those of the Korah, Asaph, and royal trials. All but one of the fifteen names from the Shaphan group had probability scores that ruled out coincidence. The sole exception was Jeremiah. He had a .0016 score, which barely fails our .001 cutoff. Whatever the source of the Book V collection, it shared the same composing group as the entire book and as the Korah, Asaph, and royal batches. We can infer, then, that neither the five divisions by book nor the three groupings by psalm-headings pertain to authorship. Perhaps, instead, they might refer to periods of composition, or to life situations such as wars, persecutions, or the reigns of Judah's final kings.

It appears likely that the Shaphan group wrote most of the book of Psalms. Almost certainly there are additional authors we have not yet uncovered, but these fifteen are fifteen more than anyone else has ever discovered, and so we begin with them. In 621 BCE, workmen found "the book of the law" while repairing the temple. In Josiah's court at the time were Shaphan and his son Ahikam, along with Micaiah and his son Achbor. These four are on the list of fifteen as is Azaliah, Shaphan's father. This evidence indicates that the oldest members of the group that wrote Psalms are Azaliah, Micaiah, and Shaphan himself. In 621, Micaiah and Shaphan were fathers and Azaliah was a grandfather. Considering that

---

5. Sarna, "Psalms," 1309.

The Shaphan Group

King Josiah took the throne in 640, a date of about 625 seems as good a year as any to fix the earliest date of composition for any psalm. This would allow nearly forty years of the monarchy to provide a backdrop for the eighty-one psalms with a David heading. (An enthronement in Jerusalem during the Cyrus revolt might also have inspired royal psalms.)

The Cyrus possibility helps to set an ending date for the book. Scripture contains 999 biblical anagrams for "Cyrus," and the book of Psalms, with thirty-two BAs, has more than its proportionate share. The probability of coincidentally finding so many Cyrus BAs within that book is essentially zero.[6] Because of BAs, Pss 8, 110, and 129 stand by themselves as related to Cyrus, but even more important than these is an entire family of psalms that announce Cyrus as their subject. Psalms 120–34 begin with the words שִׁיר הַמַּעֲלוֹת, which the NRSV translates as "A Song of Ascents." הַמַּעֲלוֹת contains the letters תהמל, an athbash anagram for "Cyrus." (Psalm 121 is a possible exception. The Leningrad text lacks ה, but several other versions include it and so complete the Cyrus BA.) These fifteen ascent psalms could even have been bulletins about the revolt's progress and the rebuilding of Jerusalem's defenses.

Psalm 110 has two Cyrus BAs and also features Melchizedek, the mythical king of Salem who blesses Abraham near what probably was Jerusalem. We believe that this book's second chapter establishes the fact that Melchizedek and Cyrus are one and the same. The Persian first surfaces in Scripture in the late 570s, which helps us assign an ending date to the book of Psalms. Another late psalm is number 90, in which the eighty-year-old Shaphan bemoans God's wrath. We have previously reasoned that Shaphan wrote Psalm 90 between 570 and 565. The span during which the Shaphan group composed the book of Psalms, then, would be about 625 to 565 BCE.

Writing One-Third of the Hebrew Bible

The same 625 to 565 BCE period would also be the span of years during which the Shaphan group wrote the flower of Old Testament literature. And how much does that include? Appendix 1 lays it out: up to 331

---

6. The chi-square proportions are 32 / 967 and 19,479 / 286,017. $P = 4.11 \times 10^{-5}$. The first proportion consists of Cyrus BAs in Psalms and in the balance of Scripture, while the second has the same categories for text words.

chapters of the 929-chapter Bible—more than one-third of Scripture! Remember, too, that this is conservative. It includes only whole chapters with statistically significant groups of coded spellings. Partial chapters have not been considered, nor have texts with improbable concentrations of anagrams. For illustration, table 5.5, excerpted from appendix 1, includes a few chapters from Numbers, Deuteronomy, and Joshua. Three of the center columns list the number of coded signature groups, chapter text words, and chi-square values. At the far right are abbreviations of Shaphan-group names coded within those chapters. Most, though not all, chapters in the appendix feature long strings of name abbreviations. This means that, in many cases, groups rather than individuals composed Hebrew Scripture.

TABLE 5.5
The Shaphan Group's Coded Chapters in Scripture
(Excerpt from Appendix 1)

	Coded Groups	Text Words	Chi Sqr	Type	Shaphan Members
Num 28	40	348	.004581	3	A,Ah,Ar,Az,B,D,E,El,G,H,J,Jr,Jz,M,S
Num 29	101	420	.000000	1	A,Ah,Ar,Az,B,D,E,El,G,H,J,Jr,Jz,M,S
Num 36	43	212	.000000	1	A,Ah,Ar,Az,B,D,E,El,G,H,J,Jr,Jz,M,S
Deut 7	6	412	.004036	4	D
Deut 33	40	336	.002319	3	A,Ah,Ar,Az,B,D,E,El,G,H,J,Jr,Jz,M
Josh 12	43	248	.000000	1	A,Ah,Ar,Az,B,D,E,El,G,H,J,Jr,Jz,S
Josh 13	90	439	.000000	1	A,Ah,Ar,Az,B,D,E,El,G,H,J,Jr,Jz,M,S

The Book of Isaiah

As the full appendix shows, the Shaphan group was deeply involved with the book of Isaiah. Its members wrote or were the subjects of half or more of the chapters of so-called First Isaiah (1–39), Second Isaiah (40–55), and Third Isaiah (56–66). There is a surprisingly even distribution among Isaiah's three parts. This and the multiplicity of coded names within chapters indicate that the Isaiah corpus was in the group's possession for an extended period, and that all fifteen writers applied their talents to it. The group generated about two thousand significant spelling groups within Isaiah's sixty-six chapters. It is instructive to see which of the members led in which Isaiah section. Table 5.6 tells as much as has ever been known about the book's authorship.

TABLE 5.6
Rank in Book of Isaiah Using Coded Groups among Fifteen Shaphan Members

Isa 1–39	Isa 40–55	Isa 56–66	Isa 1–66
Jozadak	Jozadak	Gemariah	Jozadak
Azaliah	Daniel	Azaliah	Azaliah
Ahikam	Asaiah	Jeremiah	Daniel
Micaiah	Micaiah	Elasah	Micaiah
Baruch	Azaliah	Jacob	Gemariah

Jozadak, son of the high priest slain after Jerusalem's fall, leads his fourteen Shaphan-group colleagues in coded signature groups within the whole Isaiah text.[7] Jozadak ranked first in both the First and Second Isaiah chapters, and made an average contribution to Third Isaiah. Jozadak must have had lengthy experience in drafting Scripture before his exile in 586 BCE, and so it seems reasonable that Isa 1–39 was penned during the later monarchy, with many of the chapters coming from Shaphan's father Azaliah. He was second, fifth, and second, respectively, among the Isaiah segments. Ahikam, one of Shaphan's sons, was third in coded groups within the thirty-nine-chapter opening section of Isaiah, and Micaiah and Baruch also led. Both were known scribes.

Within Second Isaiah chapters, surprisingly Jozadak again placed first. Daniel and Asaiah ranked second and third, though this might have been because they were subjects rather than authors of the chapters. We can assume that Daniel's career in Babylon would have been watched closely by the exilic community. As to Asaiah, an official under Josiah, there is reason to suspect that he was a military leader during the Cyrus

---

7. These rankings come from a canvass of all chapters for the fifteen pairs of names in the Shaphan group. Appendix 1 contains that data for only about half of the Isaiah chapters.

revolt. Jacob, our favorite for Second Isaiah, is notable by his absence from the top five.[8] (He ranked seventh of fifteen.) But given Jozadak's pre-eminence, he must also become a candidate for the Second-Isaiah title.

Remarkably, one person is missing from our Isaiah table. That person is Shaphan, Secretary to King Josiah. Shaphan became the central figure in our search for the Dtr. Coded-spelling probabilities supported that he, his family, and several associates (Micaiah, Achbor, Asaiah) joined three prophets (Huldah, Jacob, Jeremiah) and several others (Ezra, Jozadak, Daniel, Baruch) to rework the Bible's history books, and beyond that to give us far more Scripture than we imagined possible. Among the fifteen authors of Isaiah's three sections, Shaphan ranked fifteenth, fifteenth, and fourteenth, respectively. Overall, he had less than half as many coding groups as Jozadak, the leader. A likely answer was that Shaphan oversaw and coordinated the work that others performed, or perhaps as the years passed his responsibilities changed. Our analysis of Ecclesiastes indicates that in the course of the Cyrus revolt Shaphan may even have become king in Jerusalem. While holding these possibilities in mind, we shall continue to employ the term "Shaphan group."

Table 5.7 on the next page displays in detail the Shaphan group's impact upon those chapters traditionally allotted to Second Isaiah. It shows plainly that members contributed heavily to six chapters, while only one or two writers are encoded within Isa 43 and 55. For eight of the chapters—44, 45, 47, 49–53—the appendix has no entries at all. This appendix 1 excerpt does not single out Jozadak, Daniel, Asaiah, Micaiah, and Azariah as leading contributors to the Second Isaiah corpus. Instead, the appendix works from a collective, more conservative, basis. While both approaches are useful, they make it clear that we need far more coding data than these tables present. But we have made a beginning.

Turning to Third Isaiah, two of Shaphan's sons—Gemariah and Elasah—helped draft those eleven chapters. Jacob himself joined them, along with Jeremiah, his fellow prophet. Although Shaphan's father Azaliah was probably the oldest of the fifteen, he had the second highest number of coded groups in Isa 56–66. This plants the thought that the Third Isaiah Scripture originated during the monarchy. Chronologically, then, it may belong with the First Isaiah chapters.

---

8. Chapter 2 of this book sets forth the reasons for thinking that Second Isaiah's name was Jacob.

TABLE 5.7
The Shaphan Group's Coded Chapters in Isaiah 40–55
(Excerpt from Appendix 1)

	Coded Groups	Text Words	Chi Sqr	Type	Shaphan Members
Isa 40	46	357	.000159	1	A,Ah,Ar,Az,B,D,E,G,H,J,Jr,Jz,M,S
Isa 41	57	351	.000000	1	A,Ah,Ar,Az,B,D,E,El,G,H,J,Jr,Jz,M,S
Isa 42	52	288	.000000	1	A,Ah,Ar,Az,B,D,E,El,G,H,J,Jz,M,S
Isa 43	6	314	.000224	2	A
Isa 46	37	150	.000000	1	A,Ah,Ar,Az,B,D,E,El,G,H,Jr,Jz,M,S
Isa 48	53	265	.000000	1	A,Ah,Ar,Az,B,D,E,El,G,H,J,Jz,M,S
Isa 54	69	221	.000000	1	A,Ah,Ar,Az,B,D,E,El,G,H,J,Jr,Jz,M
Isa 55	4	185	.000970	2	D
Isa 55	5	185	.000013	2	E

Overall, the three sections of Isaiah have a suspicious uniformity of composition—each has nearly the same percentage of chapters drafted by the Shaphan group, about 53 percent. It is enough to make one think that a second group of authors might be responsible for part or all of the balance of Isaiah. And if so, why not look to Babylonia to find them? For example, by tradition, Jews exiled with Jehoiachin established themselves in Nehardea on the Euphrates.[9] (The town became famous as a center of Jewish scholarship.) Shaphan group members would have known those early settlers personally. One can envision groups of writers at Nehardea or Jerusalem composing new Isaiah chapters in response to previous chapters and then circulating them to others. We have accounted for only thirty-five Isaiah chapters thus far and someone wrote the other thirty-one. Perhaps further decoding work can identify them.

Within the book of Isaiah, the group's members were responsible for oracles against foreign nations in Isaiah chapters 13, 17, 18, and 21–23. Appendix 1 shows that the Shaphan group also composed similar chapters in the books of Jeremiah (46 and 47) and Ezekiel (27 and 30).

---

9. Gilat, "Nehardea," 935.

The Shaphan Group's Prodigious Output

Interestingly, the group contributed only two other chapters to Jeremiah's text, one of which (Jer 10) was due solely to heavy encoding of that prophet's own name. For his full book, we note a surprising dearth of Jeremiah coded spellings.

Ezekiel and Joshua

As for Shaphan-group coding, the book of Ezekiel is somewhat different. Eighteen of Ezekiel's forty-eight chapters bear the signatures of the group's members, and eight chapters (5, 6, 19, 22, 23, 26, 27, and 42) have coding from all or most of the entire membership. This extensive coding indicates that Shaphan members very likely composed those specific chapters. And by extensive coding we mean five to seven hundred intentionally crafted spellings per Ezekiel chapter. This confirms scholarly opinion that the book contains a considerable amount of redaction of the prophet's own words.[10] However, Shaphan-group coding does not go much beyond those eighteen chapters. Probability trials on the remainder of the book yield nothing significant. Still, one thing deserves special mention.

Six Ezekiel chapters featured spellings of "Asaiah" and "Asaiah-servant-of-the-king"—something that Ezekiel himself probably wove into his texts. For Asaiah-related coding, Ezek 1, 7, 16, 24, 45, and 47 are among the strongest in Scripture. This emphasis upon Asaiah points us to another area of Scripture—the book of Joshua. Asaiah is spelled עשיה and Joshua יהושע, so "Joshua" conceals an anagram of "Asaiah." According to appendix 1, Joshua 12, 13, and 15–19 brim with Shaphan-related coded groups, over 500 of them. The story line that I believe will prove true is that these Joshua chapters are about the revolt of the 570s, which was led by members of the Shaphan group, Asaiah among them. Joshua is Asaiah; indeed, Joshua may have been invented for that campaign. The revolt was a disaster and Joshua-Asaiah fell into Babylonian hands. They executed him as a substitute king—an event memorialized in the Twenty-third Psalm.[11] Three "Asaiah" coded spelling groups are embedded within that psalm, something which has a zero probability of coincidence.[12] A theory as novel as this certainly deserves fuller discus-

---

10. Boadt, "Ezekiel," 715.
11. For Ps 23's substitute king aspects, see Kavanagh, *Secrets*, 82–92.
12. The chi-square proportions are 3 / 1,083 and 57 / 305,439. P = 1.38×10^{-9}. The

The Shaphan Group

sion, but this is as much as can be spared at this writing. The reason for introducing Asaiah's *nom de guerre* is to explain his exceptional coded presence in the book of Ezekiel.

The Minor Prophets

The Shaphan group had as great an impact on the Minor Prophets as it did on the books of Isaiah and Ezekiel. The fifteen writers originated or heavily edited almost half the chapters attributed to the twelve prophets. Shaphan's father Azaliah has the most significant coded groups, followed closely by Jozadak, heir to the chief priesthood. This suggests that a portion of the revision of the Minor Prophets took place during the later monarchy. Azaliah, as senior member of the Shaphan group, would then have been in his prime. Also, because Jozadak was exiled to Babylon after Jerusalem's fall, we can assume that much of his contribution came before that. However, coding evidence also suggests an exilic date for the additional chapters. This is because of higher coding totals from Shaphan's son Gemariah and from Jacob (Second Isaiah) and Daniel. Shaphan's colleague Micaiah also belongs in that group. Probably the revisions came during both periods. Among all fifteen group members, Shaphan was dead last in coded signatures within the Minor Prophets—as he was in the Major Prophets. Appendix 1 and this note both list the prophetic chapters affected.[13]

Proverbs

The book of Proverbs holds but 2.3 percent of Scripture's text words, yet it contains 5.7 percent of its Shaphan-group coded spelling batches. This astounding imbalance is mirrored in appendix 1, which aligns coding results with Proverbs chapters. Four-fifths of them were signed and signed and signed yet again with the names and titles of most or all of the fifteen members of Shaphan's group. Given this evidence, there can be no question as to who wrote virtually all of Proverbs or the period during which it

---

first proportion consists of Asaiah coded spelling groups in Ps 23 and in the balance of Scripture, while the second has the same categories for text words.

13. The Minor Prophet chapters that the Shaphan group wrote or edited are Hos 5, 6, 8–11, 14; Joel 1–4; Amos 2, 4–6, 8, 9; Jon 2, 3; Mic 1, 3, 6, 7; Nah 1–3; Hab 1, 3; Zeph 3; Zech 6, 9, 10; and Mal 3.

was written. Shaphan group members wrote it between 625 and 565 BCE. Without the coding discovery, this book might never have been dated, due to the difficulty of connecting specific historical events to the generalities of wisdom literature. The leading contributors of coding groups to Proverbs were Jozadak, Ahikam, Gemariah, Jacob, and Micaiah.

This author has written elsewhere that an ongoing battle between the prophet Jacob and his unknown critics is spread across eight chapters of Proverbs (2, 4, 8, 10, 11, 20, 28, and 31).[14] Two passages, generously coded with Jacob spellings, will illustrate. This first is an attack upon Jacob's wife: You "who rejoice in doing evil and delight in the perverseness of evil; those whose paths are crooked, and who are devious in their ways. You will be saved from the loose woman, from the adulteress with her smooth words" (Prov 2:14–16). After a number of thrusts and counterthrusts undergirded with Jacob coding, in the final chapter the prophet concludes with his famous hymn to a woman of worth: "A capable wife who can find? She is far more precious than jewels. The heart of her husband trusts in her, and he will have no lack of gain. She does him good, and not harm, all the days of her life" (Prov 31:1–3). In the future, scholars may choose to make the Jacob controversy a starting point for their Proverbs examinations.

Job and Songs

The same people who wrote the book of Proverbs also did their work in Job. Ahikam, Gemariah, Jozadak, Micaiah, and Jacob occupy the first five places (out of fifteen) in Proverbs, just as they did in Job, though they rank in slightly different order. About 40 percent of Job's chapters have significant numbers of coding groups by the fifteen Shaphan members, and another 25 percent conceal a significant variety of coded spellings for individual members. In all, close to two-thirds of the Job text is so marked. This author finds no distinctive patterns in the Shaphan coded chapters, though someone more expert in the book could perhaps do so. Speakers in chapters coded with the full fifteen Shaphan members run Eliphaz-Job-Job-Job-Eliphaz-Bildad-Job-Zophar-Job-Job-Job-Lord-Lord-Lord-Lord (chapters 4, 10, 12, 14, 15, 18–20, 23, 28, 29, and 38–41). Chapters with exceptional concentrations of a single member's name seem almost

---

14. See "The Struggle in Proverbs" in Kavanagh, *Exilic Code*, 144–48.

The Shaphan Group

random: Ezra, Daniel, Gemariah, Azariah, Jacob, Ahikam, Gemariah, Jozadak, Ezra, Asaiah, and Jozadak (chapters 2, 5, 9, 11, 16, 17, 21, 24, 26, 30, and 36). It is no small thing to establish the date of the book of Job. On the basis of linguistic evidence, scholars will be comfortable with our seventh-sixth century finding.[15] What is most notable is that Job should be added to the already impressive bibliography of the Shaphan group.

Song of Songs is yet another book by the fifteen. Songs consists of eight chapters, six of which are by the collective membership of the Shaphan group. Chapters 1 and 8 are not by them, and presumably were added later. The text as a whole conceals 214 coded groups apportioned to from nine to fourteen of the individual members, depending on the chapter. This coding concentration cannot be coincidental.[16] Writers who took the lead in composing are Gemariah and Micaiah, the same ones who worked in Proverbs and Job. But unlike those books, Songs also had Asaiah, Baruch, and Daniel as leaders in coding groups. Scholars have been unable to identify the authors of Song of Songs, and are split as to whether the book is pre- or post-exilic.[17] We are glad to shed light on these questions.

As to the book of Lamentations, chapters 4 and 5 are by the Shaphan group, and there is no statistical reason to attribute any of that text solely to Jeremiah, who is sometimes thought to be the author.

Daniel and Chronicles

A comparison of the MT of Daniel and various Aramaic fragments found at Qumran shows that the Aramaic in Daniel is much earlier than that used during the second century BCE. It seems to follow that much of the book itself was written when the Bible says it was—in the time of Daniel, which was during the Exile.[18] This is supported by coded spellings in Dan 2–5 and 7–12. Indeed, chapters 2–5, 8, and 11 were written with the participation of all, or all but one, of the fifteen Shaphan-group members. The entire book contains 761 statistically significant coded groups. The

---

15. Crenshaw, "Job," 863.

16. The probability of 214 coded groups appearing in 1,251 words of Scripture is, for practical purposes, zero. The chi-square proportions are 214 / 21,760 and 1,251 / 304,245. $P = 9.54 \times 10^{-34}$.

17. Murphy, "Songs," 150.

18. Brantley, "Biblical Integrity," 25–30.

The Shaphan Group's Prodigious Output

probability that this many groups could appear in Daniel by chance has fifty-two zeros to the right of the decimal.[19]

Given such broad coding support, the matter of which individual had the most coding groups becomes less important. Nevertheless, Jacob, Ezra, Baruch, and Huldah ranked one through four with groups in the lower 60s. Jozadak, Elasah, Gemariah, Achbor, and Daniel himself are in the 50s, and Shaphan and Ahikam reach the high 40s.

The book of Daniel contains much apocalyptic and miraculous material. Moreover, since the nineteenth century, many have thought that the latter half of the book dates from the Maccabean period. Whichever way these discussions go, they must now take as proven that the bulk of the book of Daniel is awash in sixth-century coding. When assigning a date to Daniel, the powerful exilic coding should be considered alongside the early character of the Aramaic.

The books of Esther and Ruth each contain a single chapter with significant Shaphan-group coding in it. Esther clearly was written well after the Exile and Ruth may have been. The probabilities are such that neither chapter could have been coincidentally encoded, so the authors appear to be keeping alive the secrets about Shaphan and his colleagues. The sixty-five chapters in Chronicles are somewhat different. Appendix 1 shows that about a dozen of those chapters contain statistically supported stand-alone coding of the fifteen writers. Perhaps the chapters were written earlier than is generally assumed, though it is more likely that the authors were restating their own version of exilic events. When we get valid coding for those other Chronicles chapters we should have a better reading on when they were written. Taken as a whole, Chronicles stands 60 percent above the coincidence level set by nonsense words, so we need to take this Shaphan coding seriously.

About half the chapters in the Ezra-Nehemiah books are heavily encoded with Shaphan-group names, and without a doubt they were composed well after Shaphan and his team had finished work. The coding is real, not coincidental, so we must acknowledge this new fact: biblical authors used coding not just to convey present happenings but also to evoke past events.

---

19. The chi-square proportions are 761 / 21,213 and 5,924 / 299,572. $P = 1.02 \times 10^{-53}$. The first proportion is the number of coded groups in Daniel over the number in the rest of Scripture, and the second is text words in the same categories.

The Shaphan Group

This writer counted the number of coded groups in HS for the fifteen members of Shaphan's group.[20] The group totals show a notable equality of effort among those worthies. Shaphan's colleague Micaiah had the most groups (1,677), while two of Shaphan's sons—Ahikam and Gemariah—rounded out the top three. Jeremiah, Shaphan himself, and Micaiah's son Achbor had the fewest, though their totals were still not far below the mean of 1,465 groups. Eleven of the fifteen members were within one standard deviation of that mean. This reinforces that the group which wrote so much of Hebrew Scripture worked closely together—and for a period of years.

This book has presented many lists and tables, as well as citing figures galore. It is a different approach to Scripture than the one normally taken. The writer hopes that readers agree the results justify this method of proceeding. Behind all the percentages, probabilities, and chi-square outcomes is one truth—Scripture was written by people, frequently by individuals in extreme circumstances. Here are two examples.

The Twenty-third Psalm, the most-beloved text in the Hebrew Bible, is signed by fourteen of the fifteen members of Shaphan's group. Although short, the psalm still contains eighteen separate coded groups—a number that cannot be coincidental. Despite many hands in the composition, the psalmist speaks as a single individual. That person is surrounded by enemies, is in imminent danger, and faces probable death.

Psalm 23 is about a substitute king in Babylon.[21] In Assyrian and Babylonian usage, a substitute was picked after certain types of eclipses to assume the evil omens that otherwise would attach to the reigning king. After forced drinking, the substitute was made to kneel before the sun god and swear to accept the true king's fate. During a brief reign—one hundred days or fewer—he was clothed as a king, paraded about Babylon City, set upon a throne, had curse tablets sewn into his clothes, hosted nightly banquets, and was guarded by a retinue of several hundred men. At a convenient time, the authorities beheaded him and killed his family. After a royal funeral, they interred the victim alongside other former substitutes.

---

20. The total was 21,974 significant groups of spellings. This counted only pairs of encoded names for each of the fifteen (like "Shaphan" and "Shaphan the scribe"). To minimize random spellings, the total excluded values that fell below the average nonsense-word line.

21. For an explanation of Ps 23 and substitute kings, see Kavanagh, *Secrets*, 82–92.

In the psalm itself, the Lord is the shepherd, not the king of Babylon (who was often portrayed as a shepherd). "Still waters" could have been the canal that ran through the city and "paths of righteousness" might have been Babylon's Processional Way. "Prepare a table" described the special table made for each substitute and "in the presence of my enemies" told of his armed guards. The "valley of the shadow of death" probably meant the approaches to the Ishtar Gate, a death trap for assaulting forces. (The mock king's inauguration march led through that gate.) The substitute was indeed anointed with oil, and then forced to down wine from an overflowing cup to ease the oath-taking. "Rod" can also be translated scepter. Finally, his desire to "dwell in the house of the LORD" was a wish that his body be sent to Jerusalem for burial—a wish not granted.

Who was the substitute? The strongest candidate is Asaiah, a member of the Shaphan group and the former "servant of the king" to Josiah. In the psalm, his coded spellings are the strongest among the fifteen and he also could well have been the Joshua of the Bible. Each "Joshua" is an anagram of "Asaiah," and it may be that Asaiah led Israel's invading army that tried to retake the Promised Land. The effort failed and the forces were slaughtered. Asaiah lived long enough to perish as a substitute for King Nebuchadnezzar (three consecutive spellings of נבוכדנאצר, "Nebuchadnezzar," begin at v 5, word 3, of Ps 23 and a fourth starts at word 6-3). The purpose here is not to sell Asaiah as the subject of the Twenty-third Psalm. Although he is a strong candidate, subsequent coding work may turn up a better one. Instead, we want readers to understand how the Shaphan-group writers used Scripture.

For the mock king, the situation was dire. The Hebrew substitute faced an absolutely certain sentence of death—by decapitation. After suitable persuasion, he had been forced to do the most odious thing imaginable—to kneel in a pagan temple and swear oaths before the idol of the sun god. Assuming that Asaiah was this substitute, what success had he had in his life's mission, which was to free the Promised Land and to restore worship at Jerusalem? After some initial gains, his venture had ended in disaster. The forces that Asaiah led were now dead or enslaved; he himself was soon to be the victim of a judicial execution. And in face of these realities, what did he say? "I fear no evil; for you are with me" (Ps 23:4). This summarizes the entire psalm, and indeed of much of the Scripture that Asaiah and his fourteen Shaphan-group associates created. How many believers have approached torment or death with this psalm

The Shaphan Group

in the eye of their minds? God alone knows. And how have they faced their plight? With the thought, "I fear no evil; for you are with me." The gift that God gave the Shaphan writers and that they gave to us has been Scripture itself—Scripture written out of their human experience.

This book's title contains the name "Shaphan." Let us end with what Shaphan himself thought he had achieved. Like Asaiah, Shaphan had reason to think that his life had been a failure. He lived through the loss of Judah's land, its temple, and its monarchy. He led an abortive revolt that proved catastrophic to Judah and to the exiles. The years of his long life were filled with stress and turmoil. The deuteronomistic view was that when Israel acted according to God's will, the Lord made it prosper; when it did not, the Lord punished His people. Shaphan, when he was past eighty, wrote that, "By your wrath we are overwhelmed. You have set our iniquities before you, our secret sins in the light of your countenance [Shaphan BA]" (Ps 90:7-8)—sin and be punished, and if punished one must have sinned. Yet the old man still could hope: "Satisfy us in the morning with your steadfast love [Shaphan BA], so we may rejoice and be glad all our days [Shaphan BA]" (Ps 90:14). Shaphan may have despaired, but in a way that he did not understand, his life had been a triumph. Shaphan and those he led gave us hundreds of chapters of Scripture. As God intended, they helped to shape the Hebrew Bible.

APPENDIX 1

Shaphan Group's Coded Chapters in Scripture

This appendix shows the impact of the Shaphan group upon Scripture. That impact is measured by probabilities of coincidence at or below .001 and .005, and for the group of fifteen as a whole or for an individual member. This table sets out the four types and their quantities of coded chapters.

Type	Quantity	Description
1	211	Chapter with a Chi Sq =≤ .001
2	61	Individuals with a Chi Sq =≤ .001
3	16	Chapter with a Chi Sq =≤ .005
4	43	Individuals with a Chi Sq =≤ .005
Total	331	

Types 1 and 3 reckon statistical significance by using all coded groups of the fifteen Shaphan members. Types 2 and 4 comprise individuals with a significant number of coded groups within a chapter. Abbreviations that the appendix uses are shown below.

Appendix 1

Abbrev	Name	Abbrev	Name	Abbrev	Name
A	Asaiah	D	Daniel	J	Jacob
Ah	Ahikam	E	Ezra	Jr	Jeremiah
Ar	Achbor	El	Elasah	Jz	Jozadak
Az	Azaliah	G	Gemariah	M	Micaiah
B	Baruch	H	Huldah	S	Shaphan

Readers may verify chi-square figures for types 1 and 3 by using 21,974 for total Shaphan groups and 305,496 for total OT text words.

	Coded Groups	Text Words	Chi Sqr	Type	Shaphan Members
Gen 10	35	287	.002840	3	Ah,Ar,Az,B,D,E,El,G,H,J,Jr,Jz,M,S
Gen 13	4	241	.003947	4	Ar
Gen 19	8	563	.002035	4	B
Gen 19	7	563	.003502	4	Ar
Gen 49	6	368	.003867	4	M
Exod 25	70	440	.000000	1	A,Ah,Ar,Az,B,D,E,El,G,H,J,Jr,Jz,M,S
Exod 26	65	480	.000001	1	A,Ah,Ar,Az,B,D,E,El,G,H,J,Jr,M,S
Exod 27	44	262	.000000	1	A,Ah,Ar,Az,B,D,E,El,G,H,J,Jz,M,S
Exod 36	10	514	.000001	2	A
Exod 37	79	366	.000000	1	A,Ah,Ar,Az,B,D,E,El,G,H,J,Jr,Jz,M,S
Exod 38	56	412	.000005	1	A,Ah,Ar,Az,B,D,E,El,G,H,J,Jr,Jz,M,S
Lev 1	5	252	.000925	2	B
Lev 3	6	249	.000015	2	J
Lev 4	61	542	.000821	1	A,Ah,Ar,Az,B,D,E,El,G,H,J,Jr,Jz,M,S
Lev 6	5	303	.001370	4	H
Lev 9	40	318	.000733	1	A,Ah,Ar,Az,B,E,El,G,H,J,Jr,Jz
Lev 12	4	117	.000005	2	E
Lev 15	7	456	.000363	2	Ar
Lev 19	7	440	.000662	2	A
Num 1	75	588	.000002	1	A,Ah,Ar,Az,B,D,E,El,G,H,J,Jr,Jz,M,S

Shaphan Group's Coded Chapters in Scripture

	Coded Groups	Text Words	Chi Sqr	Type	Shaphan Members
Num 2	97	341	.000000	1	A,Ah,Ar,Az,B,D,E,El,G,H,J,Jr,Jz,M,S
Num 3	66	599	.000911	1	A,Ah,Ar,Az,B,D,E,El,G,H,J,Jr,Jz,M,S
Num 10	6	382	.002007	4	D
Num 19	7	346	.000246	2	G
Num 24	6	306	.000298	2	El
Num 26	79	674	.000033	1	A,Ah,Ar,Az,B,D,E,El,G,H,J,Jr,Jz,M,S
Num 28	40	348	.004581	3	A,Ah,Ar,Az,B,D,E,El,G,H,J,Jr,Jz,M,S
Num 29	101	420	.000000	1	A,Ah,Ar,Az,B,D,E,El,G,H,J,Jr,Jz,M,S
Num 36	43	212	.000000	1	A,Ah,Ar,Az,B,D,E,El,G,H,J,Jr,Jz,M,S
Deut 7	6	412	.004036	4	D
Deut 33	40	336	.002319	3	A,Ah,Ar,Az,B,D,E,El,G,H,J,Jr,Jz,M
Josh 12	43	248	.000000	1	A,Ah,Ar,Az,B,D,E,El,G,H,J,Jr,Jz,S
Josh 13	90	439	.000000	1	A,Ah,Ar,Az,B,D,E,El,G,H,J,Jr,Jz,M,S
Josh 15	134	553	.000000	1	A,Ah,Ar,Az,B,D,E,El,G,H,J,Jr,Jz,M,S
Josh 16	40	123	.000000	1	A,Ah,B,El,G,H,J,Jr,Jz,M,S
Josh 17	42	337	.000665	1	A,Ah,Ar,Az,B,D,E,El,G,H,Jr,Jz,M,S
Josh 18	52	405	.000066	1	A,Ah,Ar,Az,B,D,E,El,G,H,J,Jr,Jz,M,S
Josh 19	116	485	.000000	1	A,Ah,Ar,Az,B,D,E,El,G,H,J,Jr,Jz,M,S
Judg 5	57	364	.000000	1	A,Ah,Ar,Az,B,D,E,El,G,H,J,Jr,Jz,M,S
Judg 12	30	223	.001062	3	A,Ah,Ar,Az,B,D,E,G,H,J,Jr,Jz,M,S
1 Kgs 6	73	510	.000000	1	A,Ah,Ar,Az,B,D,E,El,G,H,J,Jr,Jz,M,S
Isa 1	51	360	.000004	1	Ah,Ar,Az,B,D,E,El,G,H,J,Jr,Jz,M,S
Isa 2	45	253	.000000	1	A,Ah,Ar,Az,B,D,E,El,G,H,J,Jr,Jz,M
Isa 3	106	249	.000000	1	A,Ah,Ar,Az,B,D,E,El,G,H,J,Jr,Jz,M,S
Isa 5	48	384	.000254	1	A,Ah,Ar,Az,B,D,E,El,G,H,J,Jr,Jz,M,S
Isa 9	5	266	.002428	4	Ah
Isa 11	36	219	.000002	1	A,Ah,Ar,Az,B,D,E,El,G,H,J,Jr,Jz,M,S
Isa 12	2	62	.000987	2	H
Isa 13	35	253	.000221	1	A,Ah,Ar,B,D,E,El,G,H,J,Jr,M,S
Isa 17	38	179	.000000	1	A,Ah,Ar,Az,B,D,E,El,G,J,Jr,Jz

Appendix 1

	Coded Groups	Text Words	Chi Sqr	Type	Shaphan Members
Isa 18	25	124	.000001	1	A,Ah,Ar,B,D,E,El,G,J,Jz,M,S
Isa 21	4	202	.000895	2	Ar
Isa 22	39	308	.000742	1	A,Ar,Az,B,D,E,El,G,H,J,Jr,Jz,M,S
Isa 23	5	217	.000324	2	Jz
Isa 23	5	217	.000108	2	D
Isa 25	22	161	.004070	3	A,Ah,Ar,B,D,E,El,G,H,J,Jr,Jz
Isa 26	5	233	.000698	2	Ah
Isa 27	24	174	.002334	3	A,Ah,Ar,B,D,E,El,H,J,Jr,Jz,M,S
Isa 28	67	380	.000000	1	A,Ah,Ar,Az,B,D,E,El,G,H,J,Jr,Jz,M,S
Isa 32	45	203	.000000	1	A,Ah,Ar,Az,B,D,E,El,G,H,J,Jr,Jz,M,S
Isa 33	47	275	.000000	1	Ah,Ar,Az,B,D,E,El,G,H,J,Jr,Jz,M,S
Isa 34	40	220	.000000	1	Ah,Az,B,D,E,El,G,H,J,Jr,Jz,M,S
Isa 35	4	126	.000030	2	Az
Isa 40	46	357	.000159	1	A,Ah,Ar,Az,B,D,E,G,H,J,Jr,Jz,M,S
Isa 41	57	351	.000000	1	A,Ah,Ar,Az,B,D,E,El,G,H,J,Jr,Jz,M,S
Isa 42	52	288	.000000	1	A,Ah,Ar,Az,B,D,E,El,G,H,J,Jz,M,S
Isa 43	6	314	.000224	2	A
Isa 46	37	150	.000000	1	A,Ah,Ar,Az,B,D,E,El,G,H,Jr,Jz,M,S
Isa 48	53	265	.000000	1	A,Ah,Ar,Az,B,D,E,El,G,H,J,Jz,M,S
Isa 54	69	221	.000000	1	A,Ah,Ar,Az,B,D,E,El,G,H,J,Jr,Jz,M
Isa 55	4	185	.000970	2	D
Isa 55	5	185	.000013	2	E
Isa 57	4	260	.003615	4	S
Isa 58	82	222	.000000	1	A,Ah,Ar,Az,B,D,E,El,G,H,J,Jr,Jz,M,S
Isa 59	88	284	.000000	1	A,Ah,Ar,Az,B,D,E,El,G,H,J,Jr,Jz,M,S
Isa 60	36	295	.002439	3	A,Ah,Ar,Az,B,D,E,El,G,H,J,Jr,Jz,M,S
Isa 61	29	165	.000005	1	A,Ah,Ar,Az,B,D,E,El,G,H,Jr,Jz,M,S
Isa 64	29	128	.000000	1	Ah,Ar,Az,B,D,El,G,H,J,Jr,Jz,M
Jer 10	5	319	.001656	4	Jr
Jer 13	8	377	.000004	2	A

Shaphan Group's Coded Chapters in Scripture

	Coded Groups	Text Words	Chi Sqr	Type	Shaphan Members
Jer 46	7	402	.000072	2	Ar
Jer 47	18	107	.000588	1	Ah,Az,E,G,H,J,Jr,Jz,S
Ezek 1	6	382	.001838	4	A
Ezek 5	48	287	.000000	1	A,Ah,Ar,Az,B,D,E,El,G,H,J,Jr,Jz,M
Ezek 6	54	212	.000000	1	A,Ah,Az,B,D,E,El,G,H,J,Jr,Jz,M,S
Ezek 7	6	343	.000609	2	A
Ezek 9	4	198	.002642	4	B
Ezek 9	4	198	.001759	4	D
Ezek 16	10	833	.002208	4	A
Ezek 19	25	157	.000151	1	A,Ah,Ar,B,D,El,G,H,J,Jr,M,S
Ezek 22	65	390	.000000	1	A,Ah,Ar,Az,B,D,E,El,G,H,J,Jr,Jz,M,S
Ezek 23	67	621	.001483	3	Ah,Ar,Az,B,D,E,El,G,H,J,Jr,Jz,M,S
Ezek 24	6	375	.001534	4	A
Ezek 26	48	307	.000000	1	A,Ah,Ar,Az,B,D,E,El,G,H,J,Jr,Jz,M,S
Ezek 27	47	407	.001910	3	A,Ah,Ar,Az,B,D,E,El,G,H,J,Jr,Jz,M,S
Ezek 30	6	342	.001962	4	M
Ezek 36	7	565	.001515	4	S
Ezek 42	50	285	.000000	1	A,Ah,Ar,Az,B,D,E,El,G,H,J,Jr,Jz,M,S
Ezek 45	6	396	.004381	4	B
Ezek 45	6	396	.002590	4	A
Ezek 47	8	366	.000002	2	A
Ezek 48	7	527	.001859	4	H
Ezek 48	7	527	.004503	4	E
Hos 5	5	179	.000033	2	Jz
Hos 6	20	104	.000028	1	Ah,Ar,Az,B,D,G,H,J,Jr,M,S
Hos 8	26	154	.000034	1	A,Ah,Ar,Az,B,D,El,G,J,Jr,Jz,M
Hos 9	35	213	.000003	1	A,Ah,Ar,Az,B,El,G,H,J,Jr,Jz,M
Hos 10	32	201	.000018	1	A,Ah,Ar,Az,B,D,E,El,G,H,J,Jr,Jz,M,S
Hos 11	28	123	.000000	1	A,Ar,Az,D,E,El,H,J,Jr,Jz,M,S
Hos 14	4	116	.000001	2	Jr

Appendix 1

	Coded Groups	Text Words	Chi Sqr	Type	Shaphan Members
Joel 1	37	235	.000006	1	A,Ah,Ar,Az,B,D,E,El,G,H,J,Jr,Jz,M,S
Joel 2	49	385	.000136	1	A,Ah,Ar,Az,B,E,El,G,H,J,Jr,Jz,M,S
Joel 3	12	67	.002589	3	Ah,Az,B,D,E,H,J,Jr
Joel 4	6	270	.000129	2	Jz
Amos 2	5	214	.000483	2	G
Amos 4	35	215	.000004	1	Ah,Ar,Az,B,D,E,El,G,H,J,Jr,Jz,M,S
Amos 5	6	321	.001552	4	G
Amos 6	41	177	.000000	1	A,Ah,Ar,Az,B,D,E,El,G,H,J,Jz,M,S
Amos 8	26	190	.001748	3	A,Ah,Ar,Az,E,G,H,J,Jr,Jz,M
Amos 9	34	251	.000426	1	A,Ah,Ar,Az,B,D,E,El,G,H,Jr,Jz,M,S
Jon 2	3	112	.000803	2	E
Jon 3	23	139	.000139	1	Ah,Ar,Az,B,E,El,G,H,Jr,Jz,M
Mic 1	6	212	.000002	2	Az
Mic 3	50	166	.000000	1	Ah,Ar,Az,B,D,E,El,G,H,J,Jr,Jz,M,S
Mic 6	5	204	.000049	2	E
Mic 7	31	244	.002484	3	A,Ah,Ar,Az,B,D,E,El,H,J,Jr,Jz,M
Nah 1	23	154	.000831	1	Ah,Ar,Az,B,D,E,H,Jr,Jz,M,S
Nah 2	51	173	.000000	1	A,Ah,Ar,Az,B,D,E,El,G,H,J,Jr,Jz,M,S
Nah 3	55	231	.000000	1	A,Ah,Ar,Az,B,D,E,El,G,H,J,Jr,Jz,M,S
Hab 1	33	197	.000004	1	Ah,Az,B,D,E,El,G,H,J,Jr,Jz,M,S
Hab 3	69	212	.000000	1	A,Ah,Az,B,D,E,El,G,H,J,Jr,Jz,M,S
Zeph 3	44	276	.000001	1	A,Ah,Ar,Az,B,D,E,El,G,H,J,Jr,Jz,M,S
Zech 6	4	203	.004646	4	Jz
Zech 6	4	203	.002168	4	D
Zech 9	33	222	.000069	1	Ah,Ar,B,E,El,G,H,J,Jz,M,S
Zech 10	5	166	.000003	2	E
Zech 10	4	166	.000974	2	M
Mal 3	6	368	.002402	4	Az
Ps 1	2	67	.001702	4	Ar
Ps 2	47	92	.000000	1	A,Ah,Ar,Az,B,D,El,G,H,J,Jz,M,S

Shaphan Group's Coded Chapters in Scripture

	Coded Groups	Text Words	Chi Sqr	Type	Shaphan Members
Ps 3	2	70	.002300	4	Ar
Ps 4	15	77	.000235	1	Ar,Az,B,D,El,J,Jr,Jz,M
Ps 5	3	111	.000709	2	A
Ps 7	31	142	.000000	1	Ah,Ar,Az,B,D,E,El,G,J,Jr,Jz,M,S
Ps 8	21	77	.000000	1	Ah,Ar,Az,B,D,El,G,H,J,Jr,M
Ps 9	48	164	.000000	1	A,Ah,Ar,Az,B,D,E,El,G,H,J,Jr,Jz,M,S
Ps 10	30	162	.000001	1	A,Ah,Ar,B,D,E,El,G,H,Jr,Jz,M,S
Ps 11	16	68	.000006	1	A,Ah,Ar,B,E,El,G,H,J,Jz,M,S
Ps 12	4	79	.000000	2	J
Ps 12	3	79	.000025	2	E
Ps 13	2	55	.000823	2	D
Ps 13	2	55	.000801	2	E
Ps 17	75	124	.000000	1	A,Ah,Ar,Az,B,D,E,El,G,H,J,Jr,Jz,M,S
Ps 18	46	397	.001986	3	A,Ah,Ar,Az,B,D,E,El,G,H,J,Jr,Jz,M,S
Ps 19	23	126	.000021	1	A,Ah,Az,B,D,E,El,G,H,J,Jz,M
Ps 20	22	70	.000000	1	A,Az,B,D,E,El,G,H,J,Jz,M
Ps 21	3	104	.000625	2	El
Ps 23	18	57	.000000	1	A,Ah,Az,B,D,E,El,H,J,Jr,Jz,M,S
Ps 26	18	85	.000013	1	A,Ah,Ar,Az,B,D,El,H,J,Jz,M
Ps 30	4	97	.000003	2	G
Ps 31	45	220	.000000	1	A,Ah,Ar,Az,B,D,E,El,H,J,Jr,Jz,M,S
Ps 32	30	110	.000000	1	A,Ah,Ar,Az,B,D,E,El,G,J,Jr,M,S
Ps 35	55	229	.000000	1	A,Ah,Ar,Az,B,D,E,El,G,J,Jr,Jz,M,S
Ps 36	5	100	.000000	2	G
Ps 36	3	100	.000738	2	Ah
Ps 37	46	298	.000001	1	A,Ah,Ar,B,D,E,El,G,H,J,Jr,Jz,M,S
Ps 39	22	129	.000113	1	A,Ar,Az,B,E,El,G,J,Jr,M
Ps 40	43	185	.000000	1	A,Ah,Ar,Az,B,D,E,El,G,H,J,Jz,M
Ps 44	49	198	.000000	1	A,Ah,Ar,Az,B,D,E,El,G,H,J,Jr,Jz,M,S
Ps 45	4	160	.000215	2	A

Appendix 1

	Coded Groups	Text Words	Chi Sqr	Type	Shaphan Members
Ps 45	4	160	.000636	2	Ah
Ps 46	29	100	.000000	1	A,Ah,Ar,Az,B,D,E,El,G,H,Jr,M,S
Ps 48	36	111	.000000	1	A,Ah,Ar,Az,B,D,E,El,G,H,J,Jr,Jz,M,S
Ps 49	4	167	.001029	4	M
Ps 50	4	178	.001068	4	B
Ps 50	4	178	.001792	4	M
Ps 51	126	153	.000000	1	A,Ah,Ar,Az,B,D,E,El,G,H,J,Jr,Jz,M,S
Ps 54	2	62	.003714	4	Jz
Ps 55	5	192	.000021	2	A
Ps 58	26	100	.000000	1	Ah,Ar,Az,D,E,El,G,H,J,Jr,Jz,M,S
Ps 59	30	156	.000000	1	A,Ah,Ar,B,D,E,El,G,H,Jr,Jz,M,S
Ps 60	39	113	.000000	1	A,Ah,Ar,Az,B,D,E,El,G,J,Jr,Jz,M,S
Ps 61	2	68	.001918	4	H
Ps 62	19	117	.000712	1	A,Ah,Ar,Az,B,D,E,G,H,M,S
Ps 63	20	93	.000003	1	A,Ah,Ar,B,E,El,G,J,Jr,Jz,M,S
Ps 64	17	82	.000032	1	A,Ah,Ar,B,D,El,G,H,J,Jr,Jz
Ps 65	49	109	.000000	1	A,Ah,Ar,Az,B,D,E,G,H,J,Jr,Jz,M,S
Ps 66	4	154	.000054	2	H
Ps 66	4	154	.000440	2	Ah
Ps 67	2	53	.000959	2	Az
Ps 68	45	310	.000007	1	A,Ah,Ar,Az,B,D,E,El,G,H,J,Jr,Jz,M,S
Ps 69	7	291	.000002	2	A
Ps 70	13	47	.000004	1	A,Ar,Az,D,El,G,J,M
Ps 71	40	203	.000000	1	A,Ah,Ar,Az,B,D,E,El,G,J,Jr,Jz,M
Ps 74	34	195	.000001	1	A,Ah,Az,B,D,E,El,G,J,Jz,M,S
Ps 75	31	87	.000000	1	A,Ah,Ar,Az,B,D,E,El,G,H,J,Jr,Jz,M
Ps 76	29	90	.000000	1	A,Ar,Az,B,D,El,G,H,J,Jr,Jz,M,S
Ps 77	51	154	.000000	1	A,Ah,Ar,Az,B,D,E,El,G,H,J,Jr,Jz,M,S
Ps 78	76	530	.000000	1	A,Ah,Ar,Az,B,D,E,El,G,H,J,Jr,Jz,M,S
Ps 79	33	132	.000000	1	A,Ah,Ar,Az,B,D,E,El,G,H,J,Jz,M,S

Shaphan Group's Coded Chapters in Scripture

	Coded Groups	Text Words	Chi Sqr	Type	Shaphan Members
Ps 80	57	141	.000000	1	A,Ah,Ar,Az,B,D,E,El,G,H,J,Jr,Jz,M,S
Ps 81	22	125	.000063	1	A,Ah,Az,B,El,G,H,J,Jr,Jz,M
Ps 82	14	61	.000035	1	A,Ah,Az,B,D,El,H,J,Jz
Ps 83	3	130	.000607	2	S
Ps 84	19	116	.000625	1	Ah,Ar,Az,B,G,H,J,Jr,Jz,M
Ps 85	34	96	.000000	1	Ah,Ar,Az,B,D,El,G,H,J,Jr,Jz,M,S
Ps 87	2	54	.000827	2	J
Ps 88	43	142	.000000	1	Ah,Ar,Az,B,D,E,El,G,H,J,Jr,Jz,M
Ps 89	78	384	.000000	1	A,Ah,Ar,Az,B,D,E,El,G,H,J,Jr,Jz,M,S
Ps 91	20	112	.000106	1	A,Ah,Az,E,El,G,H,J,Jr,Jz,M,S
Ps 92	28	112	.000000	1	A,Ah,Ar,Az,B,D,E,G,H,J,Jr,Jz,M,S
Ps 94	4	169	.000151	2	Ar
Ps 97	30	95	.000000	1	A,Ah,Ar,Az,B,D,E,G,J,Jr,Jz,M,S
Ps 98	3	75	.000027	2	Az
Ps 103	32	167	.000000	1	A,Ah,Ar,Az,B,D,E,El,G,H,Jr,Jz,M,S
Ps 104	39	271	.000036	1	A,Ah,Az,B,E,El,G,H,J,Jr,Jz,M,S
Ps 106	63	330	.000000	1	Ah,Ar,Az,B,D,E,El,G,H,J,Jr,Jz,M,S
Ps 107	57	278	.000000	1	A,Ah,Ar,Az,B,D,E,El,G,H,J,Jr,Jz,M,S
Ps 108	27	99	.000000	1	A,Ah,Ar,Az,B,D,El,G,J,Jr,Jz,M
Ps 109	29	227	.003134	3	A,Ar,Az,B,D,E,El,G,H,J,M,S
Ps 110	2	65	.003514	4	El
Ps 111	14	74	.000562	1	Ah,Ar,D,G,H,J,Jr,Jz,S
Ps 112	3	79	.000025	2	E
Ps 113	2	60	.000601	2	Jr
Ps 114	22	52	.000000	1	A,Ar,Az,D,El,G,Jr,Jz,M,S
Ps 119	153	1064	.000000	1	A,Ah,Ar,Az,B,D,E,El,G,H,J,Jr,Jz,M,S
Ps 122	2	62	.002589	4	El
Ps 123	2	41	.000104	2	B
Ps 124	15	57	.000002	1	A,Ah,Ar,B,D,E,G,J,Jr,M
Ps 125	11	49	.000320	1	Ah,Ar,B,D,E,G,J,M

Appendix 1

	Coded Groups	Text Words	Chi Sqr	Type	Shaphan Members
Ps 126	15	50	.000000	1	Ah,Ar,Az,D,E,G,H,J,M,S
Ps 136	32	166	.000000	1	Ah,Ar,Az,B,D,E,El,G,H,J,Jr,Jz,M,S
Ps 139	5	177	.000055	2	G
Ps 140	21	116	.000055	1	A,Ah,Az,D,E,G,H,J,Jr,Jz,M,S
Ps 141	23	95	.000000	1	A,Ah,Ar,Az,B,D,E,El,G,J,M,S
Ps 142	23	75	.000000	1	A,Ah,Ar,Az,D,E,G,H,J,Jr,Jz,M
Ps 143	24	117	.000001	1	A,Ah,Az,B,D,E,El,G,H,Jr,Jz
Ps 144	25	130	.000003	1	A,Ah,Ar,Az,B,D,E,El,G,Jr,M
Ps 145	38	152	.000000	1	A,Ah,Ar,Az,B,D,E,El,G,J,Jr,Jz,M,S
Ps 147	31	141	.000000	1	A,Ah,Ar,Az,B,D,E,El,G,H,J,Jr,Jz,S
Ps 148	3	111	.001229	4	Az
Ps 149	17	64	.000000	1	Ar,Az,B,D,E,El,G,H,J,Jz,M,S
Prov 1	36	237	.000019	1	A,Ah,Ar,Az,B,D,E,El,G,H,J,Jr,Jz,M,S
Prov 2	74	143	.000000	1	A,Ah,Ar,Az,B,D,E,El,G,H,J,Jr,Jz,M
Prov 5	30	160	.000001	1	A,Ah,Ar,Az,B,D,E,El,H,J,M,S
Prov 7	29	193	.000154	1	A,Ah,Ar,Az,B,D,E,El,G,H,J,Jr,Jz,M,S
Prov 8	43	258	.000000	1	A,Ah,Ar,Az,B,D,El,G,H,J,Jr,Jz,M,S
Prov 9	25	127	.000002	1	A,Ah,Ar,D,E,El,G,H,Jr,Jz,M,S
Prov 10	85	234	.000000	1	A,Ah,Ar,Az,B,D,E,El,G,H,J,Jr,Jz,M,S
Prov 11	58	223	.000000	1	A,Ah,Ar,Az,B,D,E,El,G,H,J,Jr,Jz,M,S
Prov 12	53	202	.000000	1	A,Ah,Ar,Az,B,D,E,El,G,H,J,Jr,Jz,M,S
Prov 13	47	183	.000000	1	A,Ah,Ar,Az,B,D,E,G,H,J,Jr,Jz,M,S
Prov 14	49	248	.000000	1	A,Ah,Ar,Az,B,D,E,El,G,H,J,Jr,Jz,M
Prov 15	46	252	.000000	1	A,Ah,Ar,Az,B,D,E,El,G,H,J,Jr,Jz,M,S
Prov 16	51	252	.000000	1	A,Ah,Ar,Az,B,D,E,El,G,H,J,Jr,Jz,M,S
Prov 17	47	227	.000000	1	A,Ah,Ar,Az,B,E,El,G,H,J,Jr,Jz,M,S
Prov 18	53	175	.000000	1	A,Ah,Ar,Az,B,E,El,G,H,J,Jr,Jz,M
Prov 19	34	230	.000061	1	A,Ah,Ar,Az,B,D,E,El,G,H,J,Jr,Jz,S
Prov 20	39	226	.000000	1	A,Ah,Ar,Az,B,D,E,El,G,H,J,Jr,Jz,S
Prov 21	54	233	.000000	1	A,Ah,Ar,Az,B,D,E,El,H,J,Jr,Jz,M,S

Shaphan Group's Coded Chapters in Scripture

	Coded Groups	Text Words	Chi Sqr	Type	Shaphan Members
Prov 24	5	269	.001082	4	D
Prov 25	33	239	.000349	1	Ah,Ar,Az,B,D,E,G,J,Jr,Jz,M,S
Prov 26	60	211	.000000	1	A,Ah,Ar,Az,B,D,E,El,H,J,Jr,Jz,M,S
Prov 27	53	212	.000000	1	A,Ah,Ar,Az,B,D,E,G,H,J,Jr,Jz,M,S
Prov 28	32	229	.000337	1	Ah,Ar,Az,B,D,E,El,G,H,J,Jr,Jz,M
Prov 29	41	204	.000000	1	A,Ah,Ar,Az,B,D,E,El,G,H,J,Jr,Jz,M,S
Prov 31	53	219	.000000	1	A,Ah,Ar,Az,B,D,E,El,G,H,J,Jr,Jz,M
Job 2	4	209	.002674	4	E
Job 4	32	149	.000000	1	A,Ah,Ar,B,D,E,El,G,H,J,Jr,Jz,M,S
Job 5	4	205	.002351	4	D
Job 9	6	259	.000146	2	G
Job 10	36	169	.000000	1	A,Ah,Ar,Az,D,E,El,G,J,Jr,Jz,M
Job 11	4	148	.000190	2	Az
Job 12	39	183	.000000	1	A,Ah,Ar,B,D,E,El,G,H,J,Jr,Jz,M,S
Job 14	27	177	.000195	1	Ah,Ar,Az,B,D,El,G,H,J,Jr,Jz,M,S
Job 15	32	261	.003947	3	A,Ah,Ar,Az,B,D,El,G,H,J,Jr,Jz,M
Job 16	5	172	.000007	2	J
Job 17	3	112	.001851	4	Ah
Job 18	35	143	.000000	1	A,Ah,Ar,Az,B,D,El,G,H,J,Jr,Jz,M,S
Job 19	34	213	.000009	1	A,Ah,Ar,Az,B,D,E,G,H,J,Jz,M
Job 20	32	208	.000041	1	A,Ah,Ar,Az,B,E,El,G,J,Jr,Jz,M,S
Job 21	6	240	.000056	2	G
Job 23	20	118	.000257	1	A,Ah,Ar,Az,B,D,El,G,H,J,Jr,Jz,M
Job 24	4	203	.004646	4	Jz
Job 26	3	100	.000292	2	E
Job 28	46	207	.000000	1	A,Ah,Ar,Az,B,D,E,El,G,H,J,Jr,Jz,M,S
Job 29	28	169	.000026	1	A,Ah,Ar,Az,B,El,G,J,Jr,Jz,M,S
Job 30	5	227	.000165	2	A
Job 36	5	240	.000913	2	Jz
Job 37	31	188	.000011	1	A,Ah,Ar,Az,B,D,E,El,G,H,J,Jr,Jz,S

Appendix 1

	Coded Groups	Text Words	Chi Sqr	Type	Shaphan Members
Job 38	40	299	.000179	1	A,Ah,Ar,Az,B,D,El,G,J,Jr,Jz,M,S
Job 39	39	213	.000000	1	A,Ar,Az,B,D,E,El,G,H,J,Jr,Jz,M,S
Job 40	62	215	.000000	1	A,Ah,Ar,Az,B,D,E,El,G,H,J,Jr,Jz,M,S
Job 41	35	177	.000000	1	A,Ah,Ar,Az,B,D,E,El,G,J,Jr,Jz,M,S
Song 2	44	177	.000000	1	A,Ah,Ar,Az,B,D,E,El,H,J,Jr,Jz,M,S
Song 3	32	133	.000000	1	A,Ah,Ar,Az,B,D,E,El,G,H,Jr,Jz,M,S
Song 4	37	178	.000000	1	A,Ah,Ar,Az,B,D,E,G,J,Jr,Jz,M,S
Song 6	19	114	.000479	1	A,Ah,B,D,El,G,Jr,Jz,S
Song 7	43	139	.000000	1	A,Ah,Az,B,D,E,G,H,J,Jr,Jz,M,S
Ruth 2	50	378	.000039	1	A,Ah,Ar,Az,B,D,E,El,G,H,J,Jr,Jz,M,S
Lam 4	54	259	.000000	1	A,Ah,Ar,Az,B,D,E,El,G,H,J,Jr,Jz,M,S
Lam 5	27	145	.000002	1	A,Ah,Ar,Az,B,E,El,G,H,J,Jr,Jz,M,S
Eccl 9	56	309	.000000	1	A,Ah,Ar,Az,B,D,E,El,G,H,J,Jr,Jz,M,S
Eccl 10	32	196	.000010	1	A,Ah,Ar,Az,B,D,E,El,G,J,Jz,M,S
Eccl 12	48	186	.000000	1	Ah,Ar,Az,B,D,E,El,G,H,J,Jr,Jz,M,S
Esth 8	56	343	.000000	1	A,Ah,Ar,Az,B,D,E,El,G,H,J,Jr,Jz,M,S
Esth 10	2	46	.000663	2	G
Dan 2	88	842	.000782	1	A,Ah,Ar,Az,B,D,E,El,G,H,J,Jr,Jz,M,S
Dan 3	138	631	.000000	1	A,Ah,Ar,Az,B,D,E,El,G,H,J,Jr,Jz,M,S
Dan 4	89	599	.000000	1	A,Ah,Ar,Az,B,D,E,El,G,H,J,Jr,Jz,M,S
Dan 5	75	524	.000000	1	A,Ah,Ar,Az,B,D,E,El,G,H,J,Jr,Jz,M,S
Dan 7	7	492	.000893	2	H
Dan 8	52	383	.000012	1	A,Ah,Ar,Az,B,D,E,El,G,H,J,Jz,M,S
Dan 9	7	462	.000144	2	S
Dan 10	6	342	.000627	2	E
Dan 11	101	611	.000000	1	A,Ah,Ar,Az,B,D,E,El,G,H,J,Jr,Jz,M,S
Dan 12	4	177	.001084	4	Az
Ezra 1	65	186	.000000	1	A,Ah,Ar,Az,B,D,E,El,G,H,J,Jr,Jz,M,S
Ezra 4	60	403	.000000	1	A,Ah,Ar,Az,B,D,E,El,G,J,Jr,Jz,M,S
Ezra 8	8	463	.000218	2	Az

Shaphan Group's Coded Chapters in Scripture

	Coded Groups	Text Words	Chi Sqr	Type	Shaphan Members
Ezra 9	51	286	.000000	1	A,Ah,Ar,Az,B,D,E,El,G,H,J,Jr,Jz,M,S
Ezra 10	7	465	.003537	4	Jz
Neh 3	108	555	.000000	1	A,Ah,Ar,Az,B,D,E,El,G,H,J,Jr,Jz,M,S
Neh 4	5	250	.001510	4	M
Neh 5	6	328	.001915	4	G
Neh 10	7	341	.000205	2	G
Neh 11	6	378	.004509	4	Ah
Neh 12	70	471	.000000	1	A,Ah,Ar,Az,B,D,E,El,G,H,J,Jr,Jz,M,S
1 Chr 3	33	195	.000003	1	A,Ah,Ar,B,E,El,G,H,Jr,Jz,M,S
1 Chr 8	5	301	.002921	4	E
1 Chr 12	69	495	.000000	1	A,Ah,Ar,Az,B,D,E,El,G,H,J,Jr,Jz,M,S
1 Chr 14	30	194	.000064	1	A,Ar,Az,B,D,E,El,G,H,J,Jr,Jz,M
1 Chr 20	4	142	.000102	2	El
1 Chr 23	6	333	.002213	4	G
1 Chr 25	5	287	.001979	4	D
1 Chr 26	45	355	.000282	1	A,Ah,Ar,Az,B,D,E,El,G,H,J,Jr,Jz,S
1 Chr 27	75	406	.000000	1	A,Ah,Ar,Az,B,D,E,El,G,H,J,Jr,Jz,M,S
2 Chr 2	43	327	.000158	1	A,Ah,Ar,Az,B,D,E,El,G,H,J,Jr,Jz,M
2 Chr 3	47	238	.000000	1	A,Ah,Ar,Az,B,D,E,El,G,H,J,Jr,Jz,M,S
2 Chr 15	4	252	.004456	4	Jr
2 Chr 19	29	182	.000044	1	A,Ah,Ar,Az,B,D,El,G,H,Jr,Jz,M,S
2 Chr 26	59	369	.000000	1	A,Ah,Ar,Az,D,E,El,G,H,J,Jr,Jz,M,S
2 Chr 31	62	332	.000000	1	A,Ah,Ar,Az,B,D,E,El,G,H,J,Jr,Jz,M,S
2 Chr 34	13	614	.000000	2	A
2 Chr 35	49	431	.002174	3	A,Ah,Ar,Az,B,D,E,El,G,H,J,Jr,Jz,M,S

APPENDIX 2

Books of Scripture with Shaphan-Group Spellings =≤ .001

This appendix lists the sixteen (out of thirty-nine) books of HS with average overall probabilities of .001 percent or less that the number of coded spelling groups within the book are coincidental. Seldom are all chapters within a book statistically significant. But enough groups within each of the sixteen books are significant to push the books themselves below the .001 line. In addition, some books—notably Numbers, Zephaniah, Haggai, Ruth, and First and Second Chronicles—contain respectable numbers of significant groups, but not enough to be listed among the sixteen.

The number of significant groups for Shaphan and his fourteen colleagues is also shown. Abbreviations used in this appendix are given in the table below.

Abbrev	Name	Abbrev	Name	Abbrev	Name
A	Asaiah	D	Daniel	J	Jacob
Ah	Ahikam	E	Ezra	Jr	Jeremiah
Ar	Achbor	El	Elasah	Jz	Jozadak
Az	Azaliah	G	Gemariah	M	Micaiah
B	Baruch	H	Huldah	S	Shaphan

Books of Scripture with Shaphan-Group Spellings =≤ .001

Book	Groups	A	Ah	Ar	Az	B	D	E	El	G	H	J	Jr	Jz	M	S
Josh	831	56	66	49	53	53	42	39	67	74	51	53	59	53	66	50
Isa	2,047	131	142	127	157	137	152	138	137	152	114	133	122	178	149	78
Hos	258	25	16	14	23	17	15	15	16	25	13	22	15	19	15	8
Joel	127	2	9	9	11	9	8	8	8	10	8	11	5	16	5	8
Amos	218	10	13	14	21	10	14	13	13	26	14	14	11	17	18	10
Mic	185	12	13	14	21	10	9	13	8	14	18	11	13	16	10	3
Nah	129	10	8	6	16	7	10	8	9	9	7	10	7	10	7	5
Hab	127	6	12	2	14	8	12	5	9	5	7	11	3	17	11	5
Ps	3,250	229	285	194	250	215	203	222	227	236	162	218	168	208	282	151
Prov	1,257	80	107	84	85	81	76	93	82	99	67	95	64	109	94	41
Job	993	66	79	63	65	65	61	59	69	91	40	82	56	82	77	38
Song	214	18	12	11	15	17	17	13	8	20	11	14	11	16	18	13
Lam	151	11	11	9	11	7	4	10	9	14	13	11	7	18	9	7
Dan	761	33	49	51	43	61	52	62	55	52	60	63	34	58	40	48
Ezra	379	31	22	14	28	22	22	32	27	26	29	25	21	30	27	23
Neh	462	40	37	25	31	25	34	16	26	36	40	33	26	33	34	26

BIBLIOGRAPHY

Achtemeier, Elizabeth R. "Seraiah." In *IDB* 4:279.
Ackroyd, Peter R. *Exile and Restoration*. Old Testament Library. Philadelphia: Westminster, 1968.
Albright, William F. "King Joiachin in Exile." *BA* 5 (1942) 50–55.
———. "The Seal of Eliakim and the Latest Preexilic History of Judah, with Some Observations on Ezekiel." *JBL* 51 (1932) 77–106.
Althann, Robert. "Josiah." In *ABD* 3:1015–18.
Archer, Gleason. *A Survey of Old Testament Introduction*. Chicago: Moody, 1985.
Astour, Michael C. "Melchizedek." In *ABD* 4:684–86.
Ball, Philip. "Complex Clock Combines Calendars." *Nature* 454 (2008) 561.
Blank, S. H. "Ecclesiastes." In *IDB* 2:7–13.
Blenkinsopp, Joseph. "An Assessment of the Alleged Pre-Exilic Date of the Priestly Material in the Pentateuch." *ZAW* 108 (1996) 495–518.
Boadt, Lawrence. "Book of Ezekiel." In *ABD* 2:711–22.
Bowman, Raymond. "An Aramaic Religious Text in Cryptogram." *JNES* 3 (1944) 219–27.
Brantley, Garry K. "The Dead Sea Scrolls and Biblical Integrity." *Reason & Revelation* 15 (1995) 25–30. Online: http://www.apologeticspress.org/articles/266.
Burrows, Millar. *The Dead Sea Scrolls*. New York: Viking, 1955.
Campbell, Antony F., and Mark A. O'Brien. *Sources of the Pentateuch: Texts, Introductions, and Annotations*. Minneapolis: Fortress, 1993.
Collins, John J. "Book of Daniel." In *ABD* 2:29–37.
Crenshaw, James L. "Book of Ecclesiastes." In *ABD* 2:270–80.
———. "Book of Job." In *ABD* 3:858–68.
Cross, Frank Moore. *Canaanite Myth and Hebrew Epic: Essays in the History and Religion of Israel*. Cambridge: Harvard University Press, 1973.
Elliger, Karl. "Sinn und Ursprung der priesterlichen Geschichtserzählung." *ZTK* 49 (1952) 121–43.
Freeth, Tony, et al. "Calendars with Olympiad Display and Eclipse Prediction on the Antikythera Mechanism." *Nature* 454 (2008) 614–17.
Fretz, Mark J. "Micaiah." In *ABD* 4:810–11.
Friedman, Richard Elliott. *The Exile and Biblical Narrative: The Formation of the Deuteronomistic and Priestly Works*. Harvard Semitic Monographs 22. Chico, CA: Scholars, 1981.
———. *Who Wrote the Bible?* New York: Summit, 1987.

Bibliography

Gadd, C. J., and R. Campbell Thompson. "A Middle-Babylonian Chemical Text." *Iraq* 3 (1936) 87–96.

Garbini, Giovanni. *History and Ideology in Ancient Israel*. Translated by John Bowden. New York: Crossroad, 1988.

Gilat, Yitzhak Dov. "Nehardea." In *EncJud* 12:934–35.

Holloway, Stephen W. "Book of 1–2 Kings." In *ABD* 4:69–83.

Hurowitz, Victor. "Understanding the Priestly Source." *BR* 12 (1996) 30–37, 44–47.

Kahn, David. *The Codebreakers: The Story of Secret Writing*. Rev. ed. New York: Macmillan, 1996.

Katzenstein, H. J. "Tyre." In *ABD* 6:686–90.

Kavanagh, Preston. "The Jehoiachin Code in Scripture's Priestly Benediction." *Bib* 88 (2007) 234–44.

———. *Secrets of the Jewish Exile: The Bible's Codes, Messiah, and Suffering Servant*. Tarentum, PA: Word Association Press, 2005.

———. *The Exilic Code: Ciphers, Word Links and Dating in Exilic and Post-exilic Biblical Literature*. Eugene, OR: Pickwick Publications, 2009.

Klein, Ralph W. "Book of 1–2 Chronicles." In *ABD* 1:992–1002.

Kudlek, Manfred, and Erich H. Mickler. *Solar and Lunar Eclipses of the Ancient Near East from 3000 B. C. to 0*. AOAT Sonderreihe 1. Kevelaer: Butzon & Bercker, 1971.

Leichty, Erle. "The Colophon." In *Studies Presented to A. Leo Oppenheim*, 147–54. Chicago: Workshop of the Chicago Assyrian Dictionary, 1964.

Lohfink, Norbert. "Die Priesterschrift und die Geschichte." In edited by *Congress Volume: Göttingen, 1977*, 189–225. VTSup 29. Leiden: Brill, 1978.

Lundbom, Jack R. "Jeremiah." In *ABD* 3:684–98.

Malamat, A. "The Twilight of Judah: in the Egyptian-Babylonian Maelstrom." In *Congress Volume: Edinburgh 1974*, edited by 123–45. VTSup 28. Leiden: Brill, 1975.

Mallowan, Max. "Cyrus the Great (558–529 B.C.)." *Iran* 10 (1972) 1–17.

Mauch, T. M. "Aaron." In *IDB* 1:1–2.

McKenzie, Steven L. "Deuteronomistic History." In *ABD* 2:160–68.

Milgrom, Jacob. "Priestly ('P') Source." In *ABD* 5:454–61.

———. "Book of Numbers." In *ABD* 4:1146–48.

Murphy, Roland E. "Book of Song of Songs." In *ABD* 6:150–55.

North, Robert. "Ezra." In *ABD* 2:726–28.

Noth, Martin. *The Deuteronomistic History*. 2nd ed. Sheffield, UK: JSOT Press, 1981.

———. *A History of Pentateuchal Traditions*. Translated by Bernhard W. Anderson. Englewood Cliffs, NJ: Prentice-Hall, 1972.

Parpola, Simo. *Letters from Assyrian Scholars to the Kings Esarhaddon and Assurbanipal: Texts*, AOAT 5/1. Kevelaer: Butzon & Bercker, 1970.

———. *Letters from Assyrian Scholars to the Kings Esarhaddon and Assurbanipal: Commentary and Appendices*. AOAT 5/2. Kevelaer: Butzon & Bercker, 1983.

Sarna, Nahum M. "Book of Psalms." In *EncJud* 13:1303–22.

Seabrook, John. "Fragmentary Knowledge." *The New Yorker* 86 (2007) May 14. Online: http://www.newyorker.com/reporting/2007/05/14/070514fa_fact_seabrook.

Shamasastry, R., translator. *Kautilya's Arthasastra*. 4th ed. Mysore: Sri Raghuveer Printing Press, 1951.

Smith, Sidney. *Isaiah Chapters XL–LV: Literary Criticism and History*. Schweich Lectures 1940. London: Oxford University Press, 1944.

Bibliography

Ussishkin, David. "Royal Judean Storage Jars and Private Seal Impressions." *BASOR* 223 (1976) 1–13.
Weidner, Ernest F. "Jojachin, Koenig von Juda, in babylonischen Keilschrifttexten." In *Melanges Syriens offerts a M. Rene Dussaud*, vol. 2, 923–35. Paris: Geuthner, 1939.
Weinfeld, Moshe. "Book of Deuteronomy." In *ABD* 2:168–83.
———. "Deuteronomy." In *EncJud* 5: 1573–83.
Zukeran, Patrick. "The Dead Sea Scrolls." Online: http://bible.org/article/dead-sea-scrolls.

INDEX OF HEBREW SCRIPTURE

Genesis	28, 72, 82, 91, 94	28:4	43
1	8, 10, 70, 71, 72, 84, 91	29:26	46
1:1—2:4	71, 72	31:18	42, 43
1:4	71	34	48
1:20	71	35	48, 71, 91
4:8	46	42–44	33
5	71	43	54
6	71	43:18	54
8:19	43	43:21–23	54
10	71, 91	44:8	54
10:22	43	46	48
11	71	46:6	43
11:12	43	47	48
12:5	42, 43	48:18	47
13:6	42, 43	49	47, 48
14:16–23	60	50:17	37, 40
14:18–21	36		
14:18	36	*Genesis—Numbers*	82
17	55, 56, 71		
17:7–10	55	*Exodus*	27, 28, 52, 55, 56, 82, 91, 94
17:8	43	7:28	43
18:20	37, 38	12:11	43
19:1	24	12:17	43, 55, 56
19:31–37	46	12:18	42
23	71	12:43–44	56
25	48	16:3	43
25:31–34	46	16:30	43
27–32	48	25–27	91
27:34	47	25:25	43
27:36	47	27:21	55, 61

Index of Hebrew Scripture

Exodus (continued)	
29:8	43
29:20	43
30:11–13	54
30:12	32, 51
30:30–31	61
31	55
31:13	55, 61
31:16	55, 61
36–38	91
37:12	43
38:3	44
38:26	53
40:12–15	61
40:17–18	62

Leviticus	28, 55, 56, 82
1	91
3	91
4	91
4:26	37, 40
5:6	37, 40
6	91
7:35–36	61
8:24	44
9	91
9:1	43, 44
9:15	44
12	91
15	91
17:7	64
19	91
19:5	43
19:22	37, 40
21:17	61
23:31	55
23:41	55
24:3	55, 61
25	33, 34
25:7	34
25:24–25	33
25:32–33	33
25:46	33
26	34, 35, 36
26:1	34
26:2	34
26:3–12	34
26:9	34
26:13–15	34
26:13	34
26:14–15	34
26:14	34
26:17–18	34
26:21	34
26:23–24	34
26:27–29	34
26:34	35
26:39	35
26:41–42	35
26:44	35
26:46	35

Numbers	27, 28, 51, 52, 53, 55, 82, 91, 92, 93, 94, 99
1–36	93
1–4	52, 53, 91, 92
1–3	93
1	51, 57, 93
1:21–27	57
2:9	57
2:13–16	57
2:13	57
2:15	57
2:16	57
2:19	57
2:21	57
2:23	57
2:24	57
2:26	57
2:28	57
2:30	57
2:31	57
3	51, 52, 57, 92
3:43	32, 43, 44, 51, 57
4	51
4:14	44

Index of Hebrew Scripture

4:29	44	29	53, 93, 99
5–6	92	30	24
6:22–27	2, 6	31	24
6:22–23	7	33	93
6:23–25	11	34	53, 93
6:24–26	2, 3, 4, 5	36	53, 93, 99
6:24	7		
6:27	7	***Deuteronomy***	28, 48, 49, 73, 74, 75, 76, 78, 80, 88, 89, 99
7–10	91, 92		
7	53, 93	1	77, 80
8	53	1:7	77
9:10	56	3	80
10	53, 93	4:44—30:20	67, 79
10:8	61	5–28	49
11–14	92	6	77
14:29	43	7	77, 99
15	53	8	77
15:21	53	11	79
15:25	37, 40	11:13–15	79
16–17	92	11:23	79
17	53	12	77
19	53, 93	14	77
20	53	16	77
20:26	43, 44	18	77
22:4	60	20	80
23	53	20:18	37, 39, 48
24	92, 93	20:20	48
26–36	91, 92	21	48
26	51, 53, 57, 93	21:15–19	49
26:7	57	21:15–17	48
26:18	32, 51, 57	21:18–19	48
26:22	32, 51, 57	25:1	58
26:25	32, 51, 57	27	80
26:27	32, 51, 57	28	77
26:34	57	30	77
26:37	32, 51	31–33	80
26:43	32, 51, 57	32	77
26:47	32, 51, 57	33	80, 99
26:50	57		
26:62	57	***Deuteronomy—2 Kings***	67, 70, 73, 87, 88, 94
27:14	43, 44		
28–30	53		
28	53, 93, 99		

Index of Hebrew Scripture

Joshua	28, 74, 75, 76, 88, 89, 94, 99, 103	15:24	37, 38
		21:3	38
10:4	60	21:16	37, 38
10:6	60	22	16, 17
12	89, 99, 103	22:5–6	54
13	89, 99, 103	22:5	51
15–19	89, 103	22:8–11	68
15	78	22:9	51, 53
24:19	37, 39	22:12–14	80
		22:12	39, 50, 80
		25:22	45
Judges	74, 75, 76, 78, 88, 89	25:26	45
5	89	25:27–30	19
12	78, 89, 90		
20	40	*1 Kings/2 Kings*	74, 75, 78, 88, 89
Ruth	107	*1 Chronicles*	106, 107
		5	46
1 Samuel	75	5:1	46
7:12–13	60	6:14–15	29
		6:14	50
2 Samuel	75	6:15	27, 45, 76
21:2	60	21:16	31
24	25		
		2 Chronicles	17, 52, 106, 107
1 Samuel/2 Samuel	74, 75, 88, 89	6:23	58
		18:23	65
		21:3–4	46
1 Kings		34	16, 17, 76
6	78, 89	34:10	51, 53, 60
7	78	34:17	51, 53, 60
8	41, 58		
8:32	58	*1 Chronicles/2 Chronicles*	106, 107
8:35	37, 41		
22:24	65	*Ezra*	94, 107
		7:1	29
2 Kings	17, 38, 52, 63	10:8	31
6:31	31		
10:5	31	*Nehemiah*	94, 107
12:11	60	3	38, 51
13:6	37, 38	3:31	51, 60
15:9	37, 38		

Index of Hebrew Scripture

4:5	37, 40	17:5	65
5:17	65	18	96, 97
6:16	60	20	96, 97
8:9	14	21	96, 97
12:26	14	23	65, 103, 104, 108, 109
		23:3	65
Esther	107	23:4	109
9:3	31, 32	23:5	109
		23:6	109
		28	95, 96, 97
Job	11, 63, 94, 105, 106	29	95
2	106	33	95
3:23	64	37:21	53
4	105	38:9	64
5	106	42–49	96, 97
9	106	44	96, 97
10	105	45	96, 97
11	106	50	96, 97
12	105	51	41, 89
14	105	51:2	41
15	105	51:3	37
16	106	53	95
17	106	55:21–22	37
18–20	105	61	96, 97
21	106	63	96, 97
22:25	53	72	96, 97
23	105	73–83	96, 97
23:2	64	84	96, 97
24	106	84:10	66
26	106	85	96, 97
27:17	53	86:17	58
28	105	87	96, 97
29	105	88	96, 97
30	106	89	96, 97
36	106	90	80, 81, 82, 98
38–41	105	90:1	80
		90:4	80
		90:7–8	110
Psalms	11, 32, 63, 94, 95, 96, 97, 98, 109	90:7	80
		90:9–11	80
1	95	90:9	80
2	96, 97	90:11	81
6:6	64	90:13–14	80
8	98	90:14	110

135

Index of Hebrew Scripture

Psalms (continued)

90:17	82
96	95
100	95
101	96, 97
102:5	64
104–107	11
107–150	97
110	96, 97, 98
112:4	63
115	95
118	95
119:53	58
120–34	98
121	98
129	98
132	96, 97
134	95
136:10	46
139:10	63

Proverbs 11, 12, 85, 94, 104, 105, 106

2	105
2:14–16	105
4	105
4:11	65
8	105
10	105
10:25	58
11	105
14	12
20	105
21:26	58
28	105
28:1	58
29:6	58
29:16	58
31	105
31:1–3	105

Ecclesiastes 82, 83, 84, 85, 101

1:12	84
2–7	83, 84
2:5	84
3	83
3:1	83
3:2	83
3:7	83
3:12–15	83
4:14–16	84
7:21	84
8:11	84
8:12	84
8:13	84
9–12	84
9	83, 84
9:2	84
9:12–13	85
9:14–15	85
9:14	84
10	83, 84
10:7	84
10:16	84
10:20	84
11	83
12	83, 84
12:9	84, 85

Songs 11, 94, 106

1	106
2–7	106
8	106

Isaiah 94, 100, 102, 104

1–66	100, 102
1–39	99, 100, 101
3	14, 15
3:9	37, 38
13	102
17	102
18	102
21–23	102
40–55	32, 49, 99, 100, 101, 102
40	102
41	102
42	102

Index of Hebrew Scripture

43	101, 102	4	106
44	101	4:17	63
45	101	5	106
45:25	58		
46	102	*Ezekiel*	103, 104
47	101, 102	1	25, 103
48	102	5	103
49–53	101	6	103
49	32	7	103
53	9	10	25
54	102	10:19	31
55	101, 102	11:1	31
56–66	99, 100, 101	16	103
59:2	37, 40	19	103
59:12	63	21:24	37, 39
64:6	63	22	16, 103
		23	103
Jeremiah	41, 63, 103	24	103
5:25	37, 39	26	103
10	103	27	102, 103
16:18	37, 39	28:4	54, 59
18:23	37, 39	29:17–20	59
29:22	59	30	102
30–31	41	33:10	63
31:34	37, 41	33:14	37, 41
36:3	37, 40	34:18–19	19, 36, 42
36:26	18	42	103
39	76	45	103
40:6	45	47	103
44:1	50		
45:3	64	*Daniel*	94, 106, 107
46	102	2–5	106
46:13–14	50	7–12	106
46:14	50	8	106
47	102	9:16–17	63
48:7	54, 59	11	106
48:18	62	12:3	66
51:10	60		
51:41	12	*Hosea*	94
52:2–4	62	5	104
		6	104
Lamentations	63, 94	8–11	104
1:22	64		

137

Index of Hebrew Scripture

Hosea (continued)
8:13	37, 40
9:9	37, 40
10	37
10:13	59
14	104
14:9	58

Joel — 94
1–4	104

Amos — 94
2	104
4–6	104
4:2	59
5:20	61
8	104
9	104

Jonah
2	104
3	104

Micah — 41, 94
1	104
3	104
5:11	59
6	104
6:7	61
7	104
7:19	37, 41

Nahum — 94
1–3	104

Habakkuk — 94
1	104
2:4	58
3	104

Zephaniah
3	104

Haggai — 45
1:1	45
1:12	45
1:14	45
2:2	45
2:4	45

Zechariah
6	104
9	104
10	104
14:8	31

Malachi
3	104

INDEX OF SUBJECTS AND MODERN AUTHORS

Aaron, 7, 24, 26–27, 35, 38, 43, 55–56, 61, 82
Achbor, 68–70, 73–75, 80, 87
Achtemeier, E. R., 29
Ackroyd, Peter R., 29
Ahikam, 68–70, 74
Albright, William F., 3, 5
Aleppo Codex, 8
Althann, Robert, 75
anagrams (BAs), ix, 18, 33–34, 48
    characteristics, 23
    examples, 7, 19, 36–37, 41, 52, 70–72
    in Cyrus revolt, 53, 55–57, 59–60, 63
    in Ezra-Jozadak rivalry, 45–46, 49–50
    in prison and death, 63–64
    in P Source, 23–27, 30, 76, 78
    multiple in single text word, 30–31, 43
Antikythera Mechanism, 20–21
Archer, Gleason, 9
Asaiah, 49, 54, 57–60
    anagram for Joshua, 39
    likely substitute king, 103, 109
    Shaphan group member, 70, 74, 87
Astour, Michael C., 36
Athbash, ix, 12–14
Azaliah
    leads in DH coding, 73–75
    member Shaphan group, 68–70
Babylon, ix, 2, 4, 6, 11–12, 18, 26–27, 33, 35, 37, 39, 45, 49–50, 53, 58, 62–65, 75–76, 78, 81–82, 84–85
Ball, Philip, 21

Baruch
    BAs, 6, 31–32, 53, 57
    commander in revolt, 33, 36–37, 43, 61, 65
    in multiple BAs, 30
    Joshua and Judges author, 74
    member Shaphan group, 68–70, 74, 87
    possible king, 58
Blank, S. H., 83
Blenkinsopp, Joseph, 26
Boadt, Lawrence, 103
Book of Comfort, 41
Bowman, Raymond, 18
Brantley, Garry K., 9, 106
Burrows, Millar, 9
Campbell, Antony, 29
chi-square, see probabilities
coded spellings, ix
    discoveries summarized, 87–88
    from consecutive text words, 1
    in imperfect Bible, 8–10
    in Priestly Benediction, 1–5
    in Writings and Prophets, 94
    problems in use, 11–12
    supportive scholars, 21
    why Hebrews used, 17–19
Collins, John J., 78
Crenshaw, James L., 83, 106
Cross, Frank Moore, 29
Cushi, 4
Cyrus
    as Melchizedek, 36

Index of Subjects and Modern Authors

Cyrus (*continued*)
  catastrophic revolt, ix, 52
  in BAs, 30–32, 36–37, 42–43, 53, 57, 98
Daniel, ix
  BAs, 32, 34, 38–39
  coding in book of Daniel, 106–7
  real person, 78
Deuteronomistic History, 67
  book-of-the-law, 67–68
  notables coded in DH, 73–76
Elasah, 68–70, 73–74
Eleazer, 23
Ellinger, Karl, 27
Ezekiel, 6, 18–19, 26, 33, 36–37, 39–41, 54, 58, 62–63, 81, 103
Ezra, ix, 8, 23, 42, 56, 63, 66, 73, 82, 86
  athbash variations, 13–16
  BAs, 6–8, 11, 23–28, 30–31, 51–53, 60
  Cyrus revolt role, 33–38, 56–58
  dating, 11–12, 29–30, 42–44
  dispute with Jozadak on priesthood, ix, 45–49, 53–55, 61–62
  Jacob connection, 32
  penitence, 40–41
  prophets respond, 35, 37–40
  Shaphan-group member, 68–71, 74–76, 80, 87, 90, 93, 97, 101, 107
Ezra-Nehemiah, 107
Freeth, Tony, 21
Fretz, Mark J., 68
Friedman, Richard Elliott, 27, 29
Gadd, C. J., 12
Garbini, G., 29–30
Gemariah, 68–70, 74
Gilat, Yitzhak Dov, 102
Holiness Code, 34–36, 64
Holloway, Stephen W., 17
Huldah
  mastery of coding, 76–77
  member Shaphan group, 68–70, 73–75, 80, 87
Hurowitz, Victor, 29
Isaiah, book of, ix
  Jozadak and Azaliah led, 100–101
  Shaphan group wrote over half, 99–101
  uniformity of composition, 102

Jacob
  BAs 30–31, 53
  member Shaphan group, 60, 68–70, 74
  why he is Second Isaiah, 101
Jecoliah, 4
Jehoiachin, ix, 4, 54, 58–60, 62, 64
  in Priestly Benediction, 2–11
Jehoiakim, 6, 18, 24, 62, 75
Jeremiah, 18, 31, 39–41, 50, 78, 81, 84
  book-of-the-law, 16–17, 76
  condemns Cyrus, 54, 58, 63
  leads in DH coding, 74–75, 79
  member Shaphan group, 68–70, 74, 87
Jerusalem, 2, 36, 38, 40, 50, 52–53, 60–65
Job, ix, 11
  partially by Shaphan Group, 105–6
Josiah, 8, 16–19, 39, 50–51, 54, 67–69, 71, 75, 79–82, 84, 87
Jozadak, 44, 48
  agrees Ezra preeminent priest, 61
  BAs trace career, 30–33, 37, 45, 47–66
  dies as substitute king, 64
  leads in Isaiah composition, 100
  member Shaphan Group, 58, 68–70, 74
Kahn, David, 17–18
Katzenstein, H. J., 59
Kavanagh, Preston, 1–2, 4–7, 10, 16–19, 29, 31–33, 37, 41, 48, 52, 58, 64–65, 68, 76
Klein, Ralph W., 17
Kudlek, Manfred, 65
Leichty, Erle, 18
Leningrad Codex, 8, 9
Lohfink, Norbert, 27
Lundbom, Jack R., 39, 41
Malamat, A., 3
Mallowan, Max, 52
Mauch, T. M., 27
McKenzie, Steven L., 67
Melchizedek, see Cyrus
Micaiah, 8, 65
  leads in OT coding, 75, 108
  member Shaphan group, 68–70, 74–75, 80, 87
Mickler, Erich H., 65

Milgrom, Jacob, 29, 91
Minor Prophets, ix, 11, 60, 104
Murphy, Roland E, 106
Nebuchadnezzar, 2, 8, 27, 29, 33, 45, 50, 52, 59–60, 62–63, 65, 75–76, 81, 85
Neugebauer, Otto, 20
Nicholson, E.W., 67
nonsense words, 85–86
North, Robert, 30
Noth, Martin, 27, 67
O'Brien, Mark A., 29
Parpola, Simo, 17, 21, 64
Priestly Benediction, 1–7
Priestly Source, ix, 26–29, 74
    Aaron problem, 26–27
    composite of verses, 28
    exilic date, 29, 32, 41–44
    Ezra Priestly Source, 28, 69
    Shaphan in Gen chapters, 70–71
probabilities
    calculations, 4, 6, 15, 25, 28, 30, 42, 71, 79, 85
    chi-square test explained, 5–6, 70, 86
    exclusion line .001, 6
Proverbs, ix, 104–5
Psalms, ix
    Korah, Asaph, royal, Book V, 96–97
    most by Shaphan group, 95–96
    Ps 23, 108–110
    start and finish dates, 97–98
    strong Cyrus connection, 98
Qohelet, 32, 34
    Shaphan and dating Eccl, 82–85
Qumran, 9
revolt, ix, 19, 37–38, 42, 49, 64, 84
Sarna, Nahum M., 96–97
Seabrook, John, 20–21
Second Isaiah, ix, 7, 16, 21, 30–32, 49, 57, 66, 74–76, 82
Seraiah, 16, 29, 45–46, 48, 70
Shamasastry, R, 18
Shaphan
    as Moses, 80
    as Qohelet, 82–85
    Dtr possibility, 79
    Gen anagrams, 70–72
    Ps 90 autobiographical, 80–82
Shaphan group
    coding in DH, 74–75, 88–90
    coding in Gen–Num, 91–93
    coding in Joshua and Ezekiel, 103–4
    coding in Isaiah, 99–103
    coding in Minor Prophets, 104
    coding in Psalms, 95–98
    coding in Proverbs, 104–5
    coding in Daniel, 106–7
    wrote third of Scripture, 93, 98–99, 108
    members, 69–70, 74, 78–80, 87
Shecaniah, 4
Simian-Yofre, Horacio, 21
Song of Songs, ix, 106
Smith, Sidney, 49
substitute king, ix
    Asaiah likely substitute, 109
    eclipses, 65
    Jehoiachin, 1–5
    Jozadak likely substitute, 64–66
    Ps 23 about substitute king, 108–9
    sarpuhi, 17
Suffering Servant, ix, 6, 32, 41, 52
Tabernacle, 61–62
Thompson, R. Campbell, 18
Ussishkin, David, 3
Weidner, Ernest F., 5
Weinfeld, Moshe, 49, 68
Word Links, ix
Zukeran, Patrick, 9

www.ingramcontent.com/pod-product-compliance
Lightning Source LLC
Chambersburg PA
CBHW070913160426
43193CB00011B/1448